Wire+Metal

30 Easy Metalsmithing Designs

Denise Peck + Jane Dickerson

INTERWEAVE
interweave.com

EDITOR: Erica Smith

TECHNICAL EDITOR: Susan Lewis

ASSOCIATE ART DIRECTOR: Julia Boyles

DESIGNER: Dean Olson

PHOTOGRAPHER (beauty): Joe Coca

PHOTOGRAPHER (step and product): Jim Lawson

PHOTO STYLIST (beauty): Ann Swanson

PRODUCTION: Katherine Jackson

Interweave
A division of F+W Media, Inc.
4868 Innovation Dr.
Fort Collins, CO 80525
interweave.com

Printed in China by RR Donnelley Shenzhen

Library of Congress Cataloging-in-Publication Data

Peck, Denise.
 Wire + metal : 30 easy metalsmithing designs /
Denise Peck and Jane Dickerson.
    pages cm
 Includes bibliographical references and index.
 ISBN 978-1-62033-140-8
1. Wire jewelry. 2. Wire craft. I. Dickerson, Jane. II.
Title. III. Title: Wire and metal. IV. Title: Wire plus
metal.
 TT212.P4249 2014
 739.27'2--dc23
                                    2013038541

 ISBN 978-1-62033-140-8 (pbk.)
 ISBN 978-1-62033-137-8 (PDF)

10 9 8 7 6 5 4 3 2 1

Contents

Introduction

When we decided to write this book, our goal was to share ways to add metalwork to your jewelry designs with few tools and minimal investment. There are lots of quick and easy shortcuts that don't require expensive equipment or an extensive jewelry studio. You can get the look of metalsmithing without the effort. Metalsmithing doesn't need to be intimidating; let us show you just how easy it can be!

The projects in this book include simple techniques that produce professional-looking pieces. There's no need for sawing or soldering! We've used metal shears and a butane micro torch in place of saws and large tank torches. You can make holes with hole-punch pliers instead of drills. Connecting with store-bought rivets and tiny micro screws and nuts eliminates the need for solder and flux. The one tool we felt was worth the investment was a disc cutter, but you can certainly buy precut discs if that's your preference. Most of these tools are probably already in your toolbox.

We'll begin by defining the tools and techniques you need to create the projects. Most of them use only the techniques defined in the front of the book. We've included additional photos and techniques within some of the projects where we thought it would be most helpful. We begin with the simplest projects; later ones, you'll find, will take a little more time. Although, we've found that just because something looks complex doesn't mean it's hard to do.

Adding metalwork to your jewelry is easy and inexpensive, plus, some visual complexity adds both value and interest to your designs. So gather up your tools and let's get started!

Denise Peck
Jane Dickerson

Here's a short and sweet list of essential tools to make most of the projects inside:

Metal shears

Metal file

Hole-punch pliers

Ball-peen hammer

Plastic or rawhide mallet

Steel bench block

Texturing plates or coins

Metal stamps

Round-nose pliers

Chain-nose pliers

Flush cutters

Assorted mandrels

Butane micro torch

Chapter 1

Metal 101

When you design a piece, one of the first decisions you'll make is what kind of metal to use. The color, tone, and temper of the metal will all impact the final look. Sheet metal and wire come in a multitude of materials, giving you the flexibility of working within your price range. The projects in this book use four different metals, all of which are easy to find and easy to work with.

↖ *Loose Change, see page 129*

Metal Types

COPPER + BRASS

Copper and brass are base metals, which are inexpensive and common. Base metals can be alloys or mixtures of metals. They all corrode and tarnish easily when exposed to air or moisture, so you can expect them to change in color if left untreated. You can protect these metals using sealants (see Chapter 8).

STERLING

Sterling is a precious metal, which is, by definition, relatively scarce and therefore expensive. In jewelry making, precious metals usually refer to gold, silver, and platinum. They're quite corrosion resistant. And because they're a traded commodity, prices fluctuate constantly.

ALUMINUM

Aluminum is a nonferrous metal, which means it does not contain iron. It resists corrosion and is soft and easy to cut and form.

Metal Materials

WIRE

Each wire type has specific properties; some are soft and malleable, and others are harder to manipulate. Knowing the properties of your wire is important before you begin working on a piece.

BEZEL WIRE

Bezel wire is a thin-gauge wire strip sold in different widths and used primarily for bezeling stones. Because it is precut into thin strips, it is also useful for easy metalsmithing techniques such as stamping, connecting, and riveting.

PATTERNED WIRE

This material comes in a variety of prefabricated designs that can be oxidized to enhance the patterns. They are used to create rings, bracelets, dangles, and more.

↘ *Sterling*

↘ *Copper and brass*

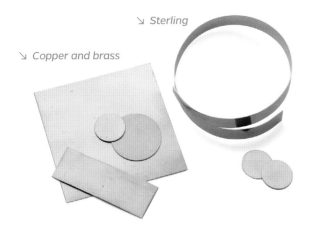

↙ *Aluminum (colored)*

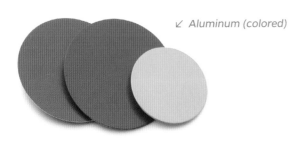

↘ *Bezel wire*

↘ *Patterned wire*

PLAIN SHEET

Plain sheet comes in a variety of gauges and types. You can usually buy it in small quantities or larger sizes, depending on what your project requires. In order to use shears to cut the sheet, stick to 24-gauge and thinner. For heavier gauges, you will need to cut it using a saw.

PRE-TEXTURED SHEET

Jewelry suppliers sell sheet metal already imprinted with a texture that can be cut and is ready to use. Depending upon the hardness of the metal, it can also be used as a texture sheet to imprint softer metals.

TIN CANS

Tin cans are readily available and easy to cut with shears. They're quite thin, so they are very sharp; always use gloves to handle tin cans.

↗ *Plain sheet*

↘ *Pre-textured sheet*

↘ *Tin cans*

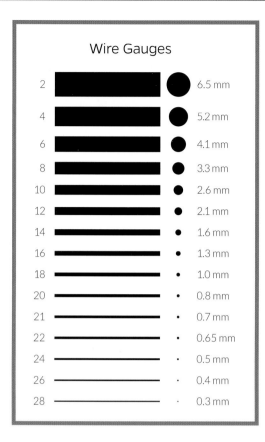

Wire Gauges

Gauge		Diameter
2		6.5 mm
4		5.2 mm
6		4.1 mm
8		3.3 mm
10		2.6 mm
12		2.1 mm
14		1.6 mm
16		1.3 mm
18		1.0 mm
20		0.8 mm
21		0.7 mm
22		0.65 mm
24		0.5 mm
26		0.4 mm
28		0.3 mm

Gauge/Size

The thickness of metal sheet and metal wire is known as the gauge. In the United States, the standard is Brown & Sharpe (B&S), also known as American Wire Gauge (AWG). The thickness of sheet in inches or millimeters is translated into a numeral from 0 to 34; the higher the number, the thinner the sheet.

Temper/Hardness

Temper defines the hardness of metal. There are several methods you can use to change the temper of metal; you can soften, or anneal, metal by heating it (see page 24). This makes it easier to manipulate as you are working. You also can work-harden, or stiffen, metal by hammering or tumbling it. Work-hardening happens naturally as you are working with your metal, so you may need to periodically anneal it so you can manipulate it easily. Also, you usually want your finished piece to be work-hardened so that it holds its shape.

DEAD-SOFT METAL

When metal is referred to as dead-soft, it is fully annealed when you receive it. It's the easiest to work with and easiest on your tools, such as disc cutters and hole punches. It's also quite easy to texture, taking impressions nicely from hammers and punches.

HALF-HARD METAL

Half-hard metal has some spring-back, or stiffness, to it. If you're not intending to work too long on a piece or texture it much, half-hard will hold its shape better and be less likely to bend during wear.

HARD METAL

Hard, or full-hard, metal is the most difficult to manipulate and hold its shape. It's best for making bangles, chokers, cuffs, and any design where stiffness is an advantage.

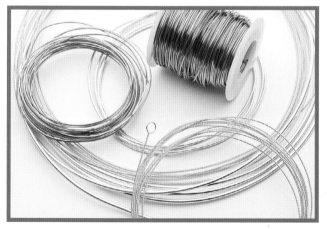

↘ *Silver, copper, and twisted wire in different gauges*

Chapter 2

Measuring + Cutting

Having the right tools for the task is essential in metalworking. In order not to damage your shears, hole-punch pliers, or disc cutters, always make sure that you are not exceeding the manufacturer's guidelines for the gauge and material you are using. All these tools come in a wide range of price points, and more expensive does not necessarily mean better. Sometimes a hardware-store variety does the trick. The most important thing to remember is to choose tools that are comfortable for you and don't fatigue your hands.

↖ *Shattered, see page 108*

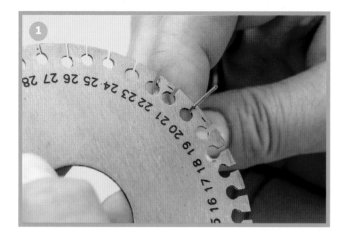

Measuring Tools + Methods

WIRE/SHEET GAUGE

The thickness of sheet metal and the size or diameter of wire is known as the gauge, but it also refers to the tool used to measure wire and sheet. Known as the Brown & Sharpe (B&S) wire gauge, this tool looks a bit like a flat, round gear. It measures the diameter of wire and the thickness of sheet. Each slot in the tool shows a gauge number as well as the size in inches and in millimeters. A pocket gauge, which is smaller and has a slightly different shape, can be handy.

To measure using a gauge

Brown & Sharpe (B&S), or American Wire Gauge (AWG), is the standard in the United States for measuring the diameter of wire and thickness of sheet.

When you use a wire gauge, use the small slots around the edge of the gauge, not the round holes at the ends of the slots. Place the wire or sheet edge into a slot (Figure 1). If there's wiggle room, place it into the next smaller slot. When you reach a slot that it will not fit into, then the number at the end of the next larger slot is the gauge of your wire/sheet.

RULERS

Jewelry makers often use metric measurements. Your rulers should have both standard and metric measurements. Use straight rulers and tape measures to mark measurements in your work. To convert inches to millimeters, multiply by 25.4.

For example: 2" × 25.4 = 50.8 mm.

To convert millimeters to inches, multiply by 0.03937.

For example: 25 mm × 0.03937 = 0.984".

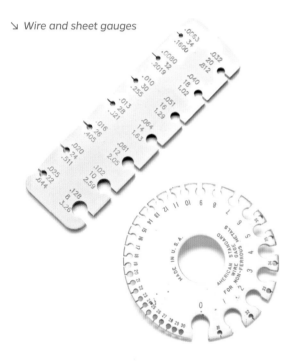

↘ Wire and sheet gauges

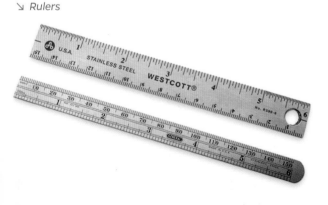

↘ Rulers

↘ Tape measure

CALIPERS

Used to measure inner and outer diameters, calipers come in manual slide, digital, and dial varieties for reading measurements.

TEMPLATES

Plastic templates such as those used for drawing contain grid marks that enable them to be used to find the centers of your discs or shapes. They're also good to use for tracing and cutting discs, squares, and other shapes.

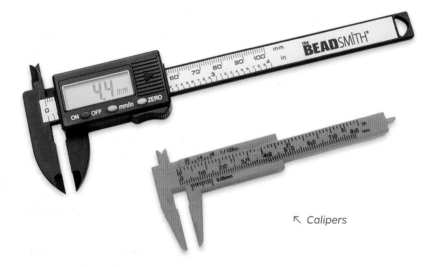

↖ *Calipers*

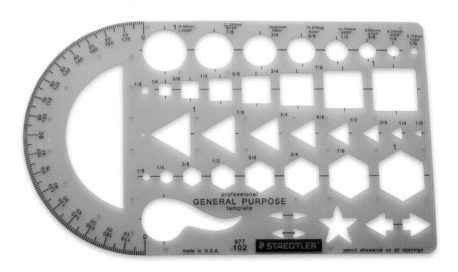

↖ *Template*

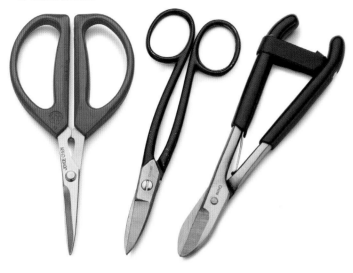

↘ *Metal shears*

Cutting Tools + Methods

METAL SHEARS

Also called snips, metal shears are made specifically to cut metal sheet and should come with specifications of how thick a gauge they will accommodate. Metal shears can be found at jewelry suppliers. Be sure to follow the manufacturer's recommendations to keep your tools sharp and effective. Additionally, several scissors brands have heavy-duty shears that are very effective in cutting metal sheet up to 24-gauge, including Fiskars and Joyce Chen.

To cut with metal shears

Make sure you use shears that don't have a serrated edge. Serrated blades will leave a very rough edge. And do not attempt to cut sheet heavier than is recommended for your shears, or you risk breaking your tool.

1. Prepare your sheet by annealing, if necessary (see page 24). Starting at the edge of your sheet, use the back of your shears for the most leverage and cut along the desired lines without fully closing the shears until the final cut (Figure 1).

2. If the sheet has become misshapen, use a rawhide or plastic hammer on a steel bench block to hammer it flat (Figure 2).

We recommend wearing workman's gloves while cutting sheet to protect your hands from the sharp edges. Protective eyewear is always recommended.

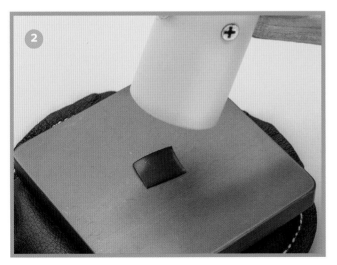

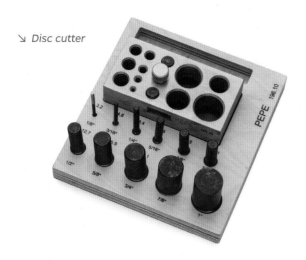

↘ *Disc cutter*

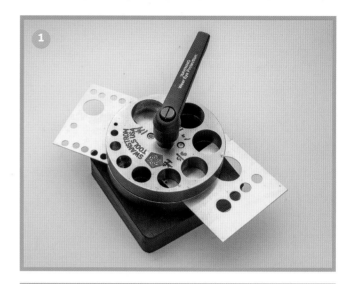

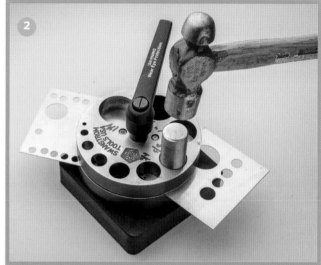

DISC CUTTER

Sold by jewelry suppliers, this tool comes with a steel block with die holes and matching cutting punches to easily make consistent and perfect metal discs. Though pricier than shears, it makes cutting perfect discs a cinch. If you want to cut your own discs from sheet rather than buying precut blanks, this is an essential tool.

To use a disc cutter

A disc cutter is appropriate for 18- to 26-gauge metal sheet. Use a 1-pound brass mallet or heavy utility hammer to strike the punch.

1. Place your disc cutter on a flat, even surface. You can use a rubber mat or mouse pad to absorb some of the sound. Open the disc cutter and slide in your sheet, lining it up with the desired hole. Place scrap sheet of the same gauge on the opposite side of the cutter, balancing the tool. Secure the sheets in the cutter (Figure 1).

2. Insert the appropriately sized punch in the hole with the sharp edge down. Hammer the punch until you feel it cut through the metal (Figure 2).

3. Lift the entire disc cutter up and let the punch fall through the hole; you can tap it with the hammer if it doesn't fall through (Figure 3).

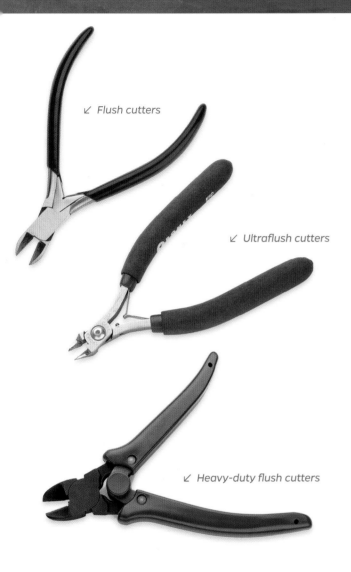

↙ *Flush cutters*

↙ *Ultraflush cutters*

↙ *Heavy-duty flush cutters*

FLUSH CUTTERS

Flush cutters, diagonal cutters, and side cutters are all names for wire cutters that cut on their side. Flush cutters imply a smoother cut, leaving less of a burr on the end. They have pointed, angled jaws that allow very close cuts in tight places. Flush cutters are sold with a maximum gauge-cutting capacity; be sure to use cutters that can accommodate the wire you're using.

ULTRAFLUSH CUTTERS

The unique ultraflush cutters leave a flat surface on cut ends of wire that virtually eliminates the "pinch" left by most cutters. This is valuable when you need an ultraclean cut, for example when you want a smooth join for jump rings. It has a more limited cutting range of gauges, though, so it's important to follow the manufacturer's guidelines on maximum gauge.

HEAVY-DUTY FLUSH CUTTERS

Heavy-duty cutters are necessary when cutting heavy-gauge wire. Most heavy-duty cutters will cut to 12- or 11-gauge. Handles are usually ergonomic to prevent pain and injury when cutting such heavy wire. Never cut wire that is heavier than is recommended for the cutters.

Flush cutters have two sides: a flat side and a concave side. When you cut wire, you want the end that remains on your working piece to be flat, or flush. It's always a good idea when cutting wire to wear safety glasses. Additionally, always cup your hand around the flush cutters to contain flying pieces.

To use flush cutters

Place the flat side of the cutters against your work and the concave side against the waste. Cut the wire (Figure 1). The flat side will create a nice flush end on your work.

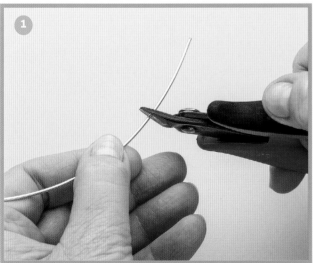

1

HOLE-PUNCH PLIERS

These pliers work exactly like a paper-hole punch and are best on 20-gauge sheet and thinner. They come in various hole sizes that match up with certain wire gauges, rivets, and screws. They're available in short jaw and long jaw to accommodate longer pieces of metal. Refer to the wire/sheet gauge chart on page 11 to determine what size wire will fit through your hole.

Hole-punch pliers have been used throughout this book, eliminating the need for drilling. To keep the punch from marring the metal, place a Pro-Polish pad or a scrap piece of thin leather between the tool and the metal before punching.

To use hole-punch pliers

1. Mark a dot with your permanent marker at the spot where you want the hole.

2. Using the hole-punch pliers like a paper punch, squeeze the handle and punch out the hole (Figure 1).

↗ Hole-punch pliers

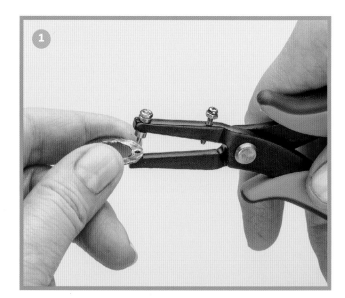

↘ *Screw-down hole punch*

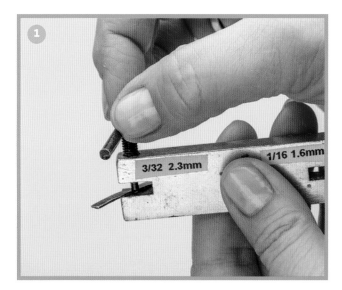

SCREW-DOWN HOLE PUNCH

This tool has two drill punches that you manually twist down to create a hole. The drill on one side makes a $\frac{1}{16}$" (2 mm) hole, and the drill on the other side makes a $\frac{3}{32}$" (2.4 mm) hole. The 2 mm hole accommodates up to 14-gauge wire, and the 2.4 mm hole accommodates up to 12-gauge wire. This tool will punch through soft metals up to 14-gauge (1.5 mm thick).

To use a screw-down hole punch

1. Mark where you want the hole, place the mark under the screw, and gently screw down until you have the drill right over the dot. Eyeball the placement to make sure it's where you want it. Continue screwing down just until you feel the drill pop through; you will feel the turning get easier (Figure 1).

2. Don't overscrew as this could mar your metal. Begin turning in the opposite direction to release your metal. Never pull your metal off the screw or you may damage the tip. The scrap should drop out of the bottom of the punch; if it doesn't, use a tool to pop it through.

POWER PUNCH PLIERS

This powerful punch accommodates up to 16-gauge metal and comes with seven different size punches: $\frac{3}{32}$", $\frac{1}{8}$", $\frac{1}{16}$", $\frac{3}{16}$", $\frac{7}{16}$", $\frac{1}{4}$", $\frac{9}{32}$". The punches can easily be switched out to accommodate the size hole you need for your project.

To use a power punch

Be sure to place a Pro-Polish pad or thin piece of leather between the metal and the tool to prevent marring.

1. Follow the manufacturer's instructions to insert the appropriate punch and die for your size hole. Mark where you want the hole (Figure 1).

2. Center the metal under the punch (Figure 2).

3. Squeeze the handles (Figure 3).

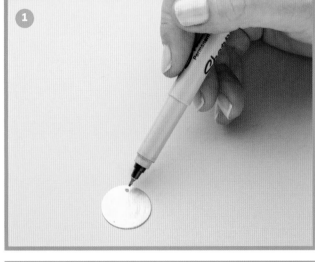

↘ *Power punch pliers*

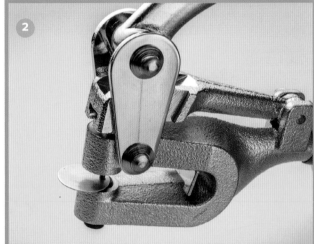

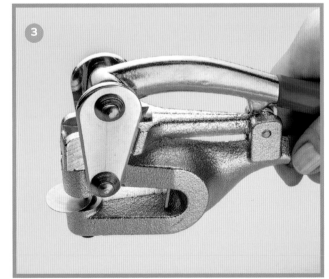

Chapter 3

Working with Flame

At some point in your journey of jewelry making, you will discover some techniques that require flame, such as balling up the ends of wire and annealing. You will also want to learn how to patina with flame (see page 50). All you need is a small handheld butane micro torch, and you will find that with a little practice, it becomes quite easy and unintimidating.

↖ *Three's a Crowd, see page 86*

↗ *Butane micro torch*

Basic Tools

BUTANE MICRO TORCH

A handheld butane torch has a fine-point, adjustable flame that reaches a temperature up to 2,500°F (1,371°C). There are a couple of key features to look for: a flame adjuster and a sturdy base that allows hands-free use. Torches with all-metal nozzles tend to be better because extended use can melt any plastic parts near the flame. Some models come with a safety switch, which you might consider, especially if you have children in the house. To protect your eyes, wear flame-safety goggles. Most micro torches have a burn time of about 30 minutes on one tank of fuel. It's recommended that you buy butane fuel that is triple refined and sold with the torch or at jewelry-supply stores. Lighter fuel may clog the torch and result in an uneven flame.

SOLDERING BLOCKS

A soldering block, charcoal block, or Solderite pad provides a flame-resistant surface for use with a torch. It will protect your work surface from burning. The charcoal block reflects heat back onto the piece for faster fusing and soldering. It is also recommended that you place these items on a cookie sheet or large ceramic tile before working with fire.

↘ *Soldering blocks*

Annealing pan with pumice stone

Quenching bowl

Utility pliers

ANNEALING PAN WITH PUMICE STONE

This handy tool, sold as a set, gives you a fireproof area in which to anneal your metal. The pumice stone is flame resistant but heat soaking, so that it helps reflect the heat back at your metal. The steel pan is also on a rotating lazy Susan base, which makes moving your piece while annealing super easy.

QUENCHING BOWL

This is a ceramic, glass, or metal bowl filled with cold water. Submerging the hot metal into cold water reduces the heat of an item that has been fused, soldered, or annealed.

Whenever you are using a torch to heat metal or wire, dip the piece in a bowl of water before touching it. Even if a piece is not glowing, a quick dip in a quenching bowl will ensure that you're not burned.

If you don't want to use water on your metal to cool it, you can place it on a steel anvil or bench block to draw the heat out of it. Cooling time takes longer than quenching but is faster than air cooling.

UTILITY PLIERS

These are everyday needle-nose pliers with a heat-resistant handle. They are not used for jewelry making but for holding wire and metal in the flame and to dip items in the quenching bowl.

MINI CROCK

You can purchase an inexpensive, small mini crock for your pickling solution. Make sure this is designated for pickle only.

COPPER TONGS

It is essential to use copper tongs with chemical pickle as other metals will contaminate the solution, which in turn affects your metals.

PICKLE

Pickle is an acid solution used to remove oxidation and fire scale from metal after it's been soldered or heated with a torch. It is sodium bisulfate and is sold as jewelry pickling compound at jewelry suppliers. It's dissolved in hot water and works most effectively if the water is kept heated. Be sure to neutralize the solution by adding a few teaspoons of baking soda before discarding. You can also make an organic pickling solution with 1 cup white vinegar and 1 teaspoon salt, which should also be kept hot.

↗ *Mini crock*

↘ *Copper tongs*

↘ *Ingredients for organic pickling solution can be found at your grocery store*

TO USE PICKLE

Chemical pickling solutions, as well as organic pickling solutions, must be kept hot to be most effective. Use a small slow cooker designated for pickle only.

CAUTION:
Do not splash the acid around and always add acid to water—NOT the other way around. Always follow the manufacturer's safety instructions.

1. Fill the mini crock halfway with clean water. If your tap water has a lot of minerals in it, use distilled water. Add the pickle solution according to the manufacturer's instructions. Turn on the mini crock to heat the solution and keep it warm while you are working. Using copper tongs, place your piece in the solution, being careful not to splash the solution (Figure 1).

2. Leave it in the solution anywhere from 5 to 15 minutes, until the metal is clean. Remove with copper tongs (Figure 2), rinse, and dry.

3. This solution can be used many times and reheated repeatedly. When you're ready to discard it, make sure to neutralize the solution with baking soda. Once the solution is neutralized, you can flush it or put it down the sink.

Annealing

Annealing is the process of heating metal with a flame to a temperature at which it becomes soft and malleable. This can become necessary as you work, for the metal work-hardens (grows stiffer and more resistant) the more it is manipulated. Annealing usually occurs when the metal glows a dull red in the flame. The hottest part of the flame is at the blue tip inside the larger orange flame. Refueling the torch before each use ensures that you will have the hottest flame.

1. Make a mark on your metal with a permanent marker.

2. Run the flame back and forth several times over the length of metal you want to soften (Figures 1 and 2). When the permanent marker fades, the metal is annealed.

3. Use utility pliers to transfer the annealed piece to a bowl of cold water to quench it before touching it (Figure 3). Clean off the fire scale if needed (see Finishing, page 52).

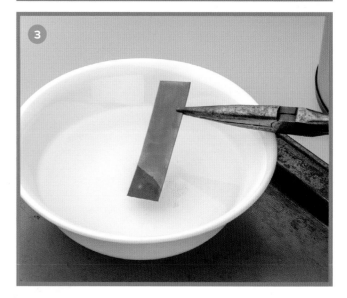

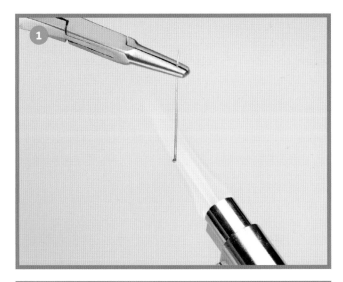

Balling the End of Wire

Balling the end of wire is a versatile technique that can be used for creating head pins, ear wires, decorative connections, and more.

1. Using utility pliers or tweezers, hold one end of a piece of copper, sterling, or fine-silver wire perpendicular in the blue, hottest portion of the flame on the butane micro torch (Figure 1).

2. When the wire balls up to the size you desire, remove it from the flame, quench it in a bowl of cool water, and clean off the fire scale if needed (see Finishing, page 52) (Figure 2).

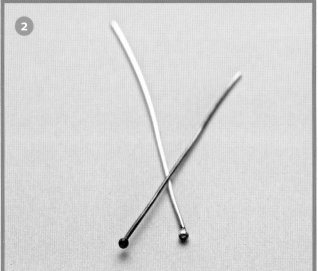

Chapter 4

Texturing

Texturing is a fast and easy way to add interest to metal and wire. To highlight and bring out the depth of any texture, adding patina afterward is a great option (see page 48). For the purpose of the projects in this book, we've textured metal that ranges in thickness from 24-gauge sheet to 30-gauge.

Depending upon the gauge of the metal, it may need softening in order to take the texture better. When using a hammer, always grasp the hammer firmly near the end of the handle. Do not "choke up" on the handle as you might a baseball bat. This ensures you're using the weight of the head optimally and also keeps your hand from absorbing the shock of the impact. When hammering, be aware that you will also be work-hardening the metal, and you may need to anneal it again before continuing to work with it.

⬉ Saucy, see page 92

↙ Steel bench block, leather sandbag

↘ Brass-head mallet, tape

↘ Ball-peen hammer, chasing hammer, riveting hammer

↘ Texturing hammers

↘ Changeable heads

Utility Tools for Texturing

STEEL BENCH BLOCK

A steel bench block provides a small and portable hard surface on which to hammer. It's made of polished steel and is usually only ¾" (2 cm) thick and a few inches square.

LEATHER SANDBAG

This sound-deadening and shock-absorbing pad sits beneath your bench block. A mouse pad makes a quick and handy alternative to a leather sandbag.

BRASS-HEAD MALLET

A brass-head mallet strikes a nice, even blow when used with stamping tools. The head is brass and therefore softer than steel. You will see damage to the flat surface of the hammer after using it with your stamps; this is to be expected.

TAPE

Blue painter's tape is an essential tool when using coins and texture sheets for taping your metal to the texture surface. Transparent tape is also handy for stamping.

Texturing Tools

HAMMERS

Chasing or ball-peen hammers: These hammers have one round domed head and one round flat head. The domed heads can be used for making a nice dimpled texture.

Riveting hammer: This hammer has one round face and one chiseled face. The chiseled face makes a very good linear impression on metal.

Texturing hammers: These specialty hammers are made for the express purpose of adding texture to metal. They have carved or embossed faces that make designs such as dots or checkerboards in your metal.

To texture with hammers

There are lots of tools to create texture on metal. One of the simplest is using the ball end of a chasing or ball-peen hammer.

Place your metal on a steel bench block or steel mandrel. Strike the metal with enough force to transfer the impression of the hammer head to the metal and form a dimpled pattern (Figure 1).

STAMPS

These small tools come in a variety of letters, numbers, and designs, and are made of tool steel with an embossed impression on one end. Used with a brass-head mallet, the small design moves the metal onto which you're stamping and leaves an impression of the design on your sheet.

To texture with stamps

There is a huge variety of steel design stamps available for decorating metal, including alphabets in a number of fonts.

Using transparent tape, affix your metal to the steel bench block. With a brass hammer, position the design end of the stamp where you want to place the impression and give a single solid blow to the other end of the stamp (Figure 2). If you have a particularly ornate design stamp, use a heavier 2-pound brass hammer.

↘ *Stamps*

↘ *Coins and patterned sheets*

COINS + PATTERNED SHEET

Coins are made of hard metal and are intricately designed. By placing annealed or soft sheet metal on top of a coin, you can transfer the coin designs onto your sheet by hammering.

Jewelry suppliers sell sheet metal that has already been tooled with intricate designs embossed on them. Hard-metal patterned sheet can be used as texture plates. By placing annealed or soft sheet metal on top of a piece of textured brass sheet, you can transfer the design onto your sheet by hammering.

To texture with coins + patterned sheet

If using a coin, be careful to avoid hammering too much along the edges of the coin as this may cause weak spots in your metal. Make sure not to use valuable or favorite coins as this technique causes a lot of wear and will eventually ruin them.

1. Using painter's tape, adhere the annealed metal piece to the textured side of the brass texture sheet or coin (Figure 1).

2. With your sheet metal on the top and texture on the bottom, hammer thoroughly with both sides of your utility ball-peen hammer; first with the flat end and then with the ball end (Figure 2). If you find the impression isn't deep enough, start with a heavier utility hammer and then finish up more thoroughly with the ball end of your chasing hammer.

3. Remove the metal to reveal the pattern (Figure 3).

SIZZIX BIGKICK MACHINE

This embossing machine was originally created for the scrapbooking industry. Vintaj has adapted it to work with their metal blanks. It works like a low-tech rolling mill, impressing your sheet metal with designs from purchased embossing plates.

↘ *Sizzix BIGkick machine*

To use the Sizzix BIGkick machine:

This machine embosses and etches different designs using DecoEtch and DecoEmboss dies.

1. Place a 24-gauge Vintaj blank on top of the chosen die, following the instructions that come with the machine (Figure 1).

2. Roll the die through the machine (Figures 2 and 3).

3. Use the sanding sponge to highlight the design (Figure 4).

DIMPLING PLIERS

These pliers have one sharply curved jaw and one flat jaw with a dimpled impression. Squeezing your sheet metal in these pliers will form a little bump in your metal. They come in a variety of dimple sizes and make it easy to place the texture where you want it. Rotate the pliers to create a concave or convex impression.

To use dimpling pliers

Mark your metal where you want to place the dimple. Place the jaw of the dimpling pliers at the mark and squeeze (Figure 1).

SANDING TOOLS

Abrasives such as steel wool, sandpaper, sanding sponges, and brass brushes can be used to obtain an interesting brushed matte finish. It is important to keep in mind what direction you are scratching the surface; moving in a circular pattern creates the most uniformity.

To sand for texture

Apply the sandpaper to the surface of the metal, using consistent strokes. Create the patterns of your choice.

↗ Dimpling pliers

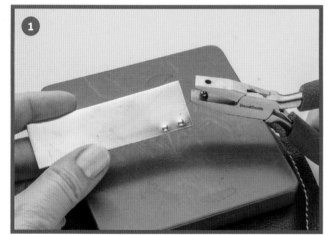

↙ Sanding tools

Chapter 5

Forming

Any manipulation of metal is considered forming. Forming creates interesting three-dimensional pieces. As you move into heavier gauges you will need to anneal the metal (see page 24) before working with it, and perhaps afterward if you plan to continue working with the design.

↖ *Silk Road, see page 134*

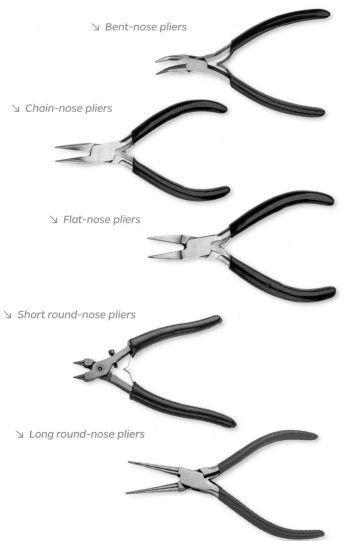

↘ Bent-nose pliers

↘ Chain-nose pliers

↘ Flat-nose pliers

↘ Short round-nose pliers

↘ Long round-nose pliers

Forming Tools

PLIERS

Chain-nose pliers: The workhorse of wire tools, chain-nose pliers are used for grasping wire and sheet, opening and closing jump rings, and making sharp angled bends. Because you may need to manipulate the wire or sheet using both hands, it's a good idea to have at least two pairs in your workshop. Bent chain-nose pliers are similar to chain-nose pliers but have a bend at the tip that allows access to tight places for tasks such as tightening coils and tucking in ends.

Flat-nose pliers: Flat-nose pliers have broad flat jaws and are good for making sharp bends, grasping spirals, and holding components.

Round-nose pliers: Another wireworker's necessity, round-nose pliers have pointed, graduated round jaws. They are used for making jump rings, simple loops, and curved bends in wire or sheet. They are also available in short and long nose. Longer jaws give you a longer reach but less leverage at the tips. Shorter jaws offer more strength at their tips but less of a reach. You can ruin long-nose pliers trying to bend heavy-gauge wire or sheet.

Bail-forming pliers: Bail-forming pliers have long untapered jaws that enable you to make consistent loops. Each jaw has a slightly different diameter, so one set of pliers enables you to make two sizes of loops.

↘ Bail-forming pliers

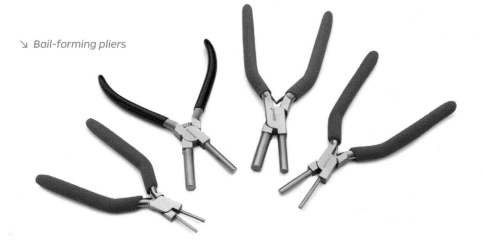

Stepped forming pliers: Stepped forming pliers come in different sizes and shapes. They can have one flat jaw or one concave jaw and one jaw of various-sized round barrels. They're perfect for wrapping loops of a consistent size. They may also be called wrap-and-tap pliers.

Nylon-jaw pliers/wire-straightening pliers: The jaws of these pliers are made of hard nylon. Pulling wire through the clamped jaws will straighten any bends or kinks. They can also be used to hold, bend, or shape wire and sheet without marring it. Keep in mind that every time you pull wire through straightening pliers, you're work-hardening it more, making it more brittle and harder to manipulate.

Forming sheet with pliers

Manipulation with pliers is considered forming whether it is using the pliers as a mandrel or using them as a gripping tool to pull the sheet around a mandrel. They are really the most basic tool there is for forming.

Anneal the metal if necessary (see page 24). Grasp the edge of the sheet between the jaws of the pliers and bend the metal to form an angle or tube (Figure 1).

MANDRELS

A mandrel is a spindle, rod, or bar around which you can bend metal or wire. Depending upon the hardness and gauge of the metal, you can form the metal around mandrels using your hands or tools. Mandrels come in a variety of shapes and sizes. Some are made specifically for bracelets, rings, and making bezels. Almost anything can be used as a mandrel to shape wire, including wooden dowels, ballpoint pens, chopsticks, knitting needles, carpenter's pencils, and other pieces of wire. A Sharpie-brand permanent marker is the perfect shape for making French ear wires.

Forming sheet around a mandrel

Anneal the metal if necessary (see page 24). Place the sheet against the mandrel and begin hammering with a rawhide mallet to shape the metal to the form of the mandrel (Figure 2). Continue moving the sheet around the mandrel as you hammer.

↘ *Stepped forming pliers*

↘ *Nylon-jaw pliers*

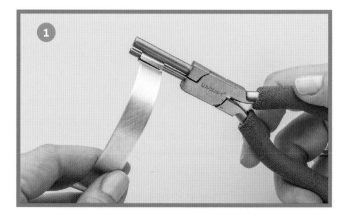

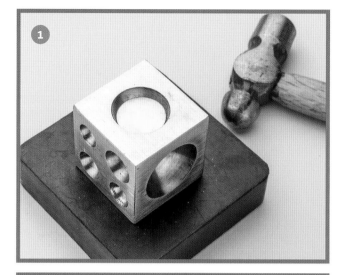

DAPPING BLOCK + PUNCHES

These are simple tools that do a gargantuan job. They come in steel and wood, and the block has various-sized depressions on each side for shaping and doming metal, most often discs. The block is used with punches, also in wood or steel. Gently hammering the punches against metal, in the depressions, shapes the metal.

Forming sheet by dapping and doming

Dapping and doming in a forming block is a quick and easy way to make concave and convex shapes in your metal.

1. Place a metal disc in a depression in the forming block that is bigger than the disc (Figure 1).

2. Using a brass or utility hammer and corresponding punch, hammer the punch to form the disc into a dome. If you are doming a textured piece, place a Pro-Polish pad between the texture and the tool (Figure 2).

3. To make the dome higher, gradually move the disc to smaller depressions and hammer with corresponding punches (Figure 3).

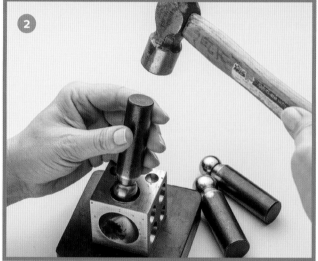

RAWHIDE/NYLON MALLET

Rawhide and nylon mallets are used for shaping metal around mandrels and for work-hardening or flattening it without marring it.

ANVIL

This handy bench tool, used for shaping and forming wire and metal, comes in a selection of sizes. Made of hardened tool steel, it offers a flat surface and often one flat horn and one rounded horn.

BENCH BLOCKS

Steel bench blocks (see page 27) are used most frequently as a hard and portable surface on which to hammer metal. Nylon and rubber bench blocks are also useful because they provide a softer surface on which to hammer, preventing the metal from being marred.

Other Useful Tools

Leather sandbag (see page 27)

Brass-head mallet (see page 27)

Chasing hammer (see page 27).

↙ *Rawhide mallet*

↗ *Nylon mallet*

↘ *Anvil*

↗ *Bench blocks*

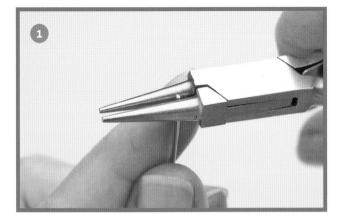

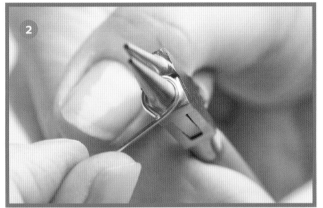

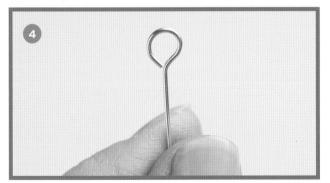

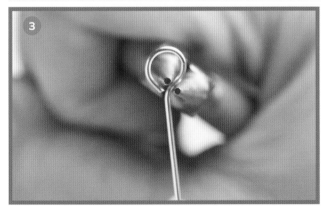

Forming with Wire

Almost all jewelry pieces include wire in some form. These are some of the most basic and frequently used techniques. The secret to fine-wire jewelry is neatness. Ends should be neat and smooth or tucked out of sight, and wrapped loops should have the same number of wraps on each neck. Try working from the spool of wire, instead of cutting a separate length to start each piece. It eliminates waste and is much more cost-effective.

SIMPLE LOOP

1. Working from the spool, flush cut the end of the wire. Grasp the end of the wire in round-nose pliers so you can just see the tip of the wire (Figure 1).

2. Rotate the pliers fully until you've made a complete loop (Figure 2).

3. Remove the pliers. Reinsert the tip of the pliers to grasp the wire directly across from the opening of the loop. Make a sharp 45° bend across from the opening (Figure 3).

4. Center the loop over the length of the wire like a lollipop (Figure 4).

Tip: For making consistent loops, use a black permanent marker to draw a guideline on the jaw of your round-nose pliers. Use this guide to produce the same-size loop again and again.

WRAPPED LOOP

1. Working from the spool, flush cut the end of the wire. Grasp the wire about 2" (5 cm) from the end with chain-nose pliers. Use your fingers to bend the wire flat against the pliers to 90° (Figure 1).

2. Use round-nose pliers to grasp the wire right at the bend you just made, holding the pliers perpendicular to the tabletop. Pull the wire up and over the top of the round-nose pliers (Figure 2).

3. Pull the pliers out and put the lower jaw back into the loop you just made (Figure 3).

4. Continue pulling the wire around the bottom jaw of the pliers into a full round loop (Figure 4).

5. With your fingers or chain-nose pliers, wrap the wire around the neck of the lower wire two or three times (Figures 5 and 6).

6. Trim the wire and pinch the end snugly with chain-nose pliers.

Tip: Once you master a fine-wrapped loop, you can double the loop, wrapping twice around the jaws of the pliers, for additional strength and interest in your designs.

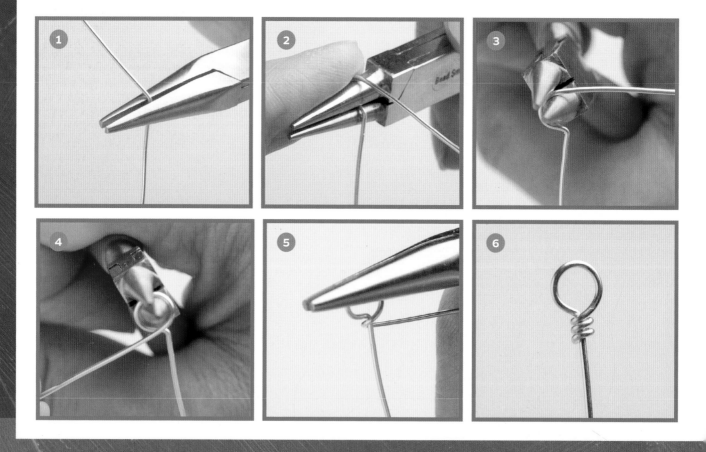

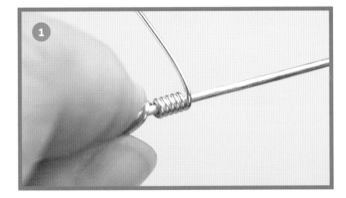

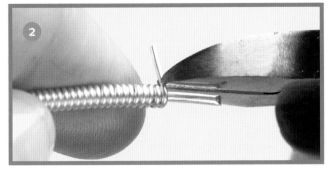

HAND COILING

1. Coils can be made on any round mandrel, including another piece of wire. Hold one end of the wire tightly against the mandrel with your thumb and coil the length up the mandrel. Be sure to wrap snugly and keep the coils right next to one another (Figure 1).

2. Flush cut both ends (Figure 2).

USING A COILING TOOL

1. Anchor the frame to the desk using a C-clamp or hold it in your nondominant hand. Working from the spool of wire, wrap the end of the wire a couple of times around the back of the mandrel to anchor it (Figure 1).

2. Insert the mandrel into the frame and begin turning the mandrel to start the coil, near the handle. Keep the wire taut while you feed it onto the mandrel (Figure 2).

3. Gently push the coil against the frame to keep the wraps tightly against one another. Keep turning the mandrel and pushing the coil against the frame until the coil is the length you want (Figure 3).

4. Trim the wire from the spool, unwrap the anchor wire, and remove the coil from the mandrel. You may need to break the tension of the coil in order to remove it. To do this, grasp both ends of the coil on the mandrel and twist them slightly in opposite directions. Flush cut both ends of the coil.

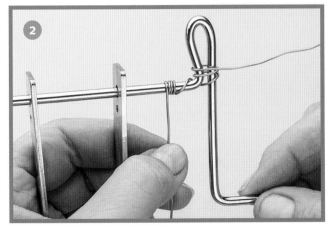

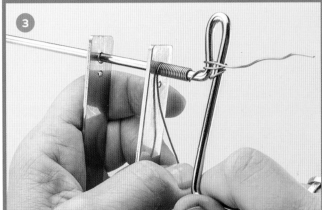

JUMP RINGS

1. Coil the wire snugly around a mandrel (Figure 1). Each single coil will make one jump ring.

2. Remove the mandrel. Use flush cutters to cut through all the rings at the same spot along the length of the coil, snipping one or two at a time (Figure 2). They will fall away and each ring will be slightly open. One side of the ring will be flush-cut, and the other side will have a beveled edge. Flush-cut the beveled side so the ring will close properly.

3. Tumble to work-harden or hammer with the rawhide hammer and bench block. The jump rings you make will have the inner diameter (ID) of the mandrel you used to make them.

4. Always use two chain- or bent-nose pliers to open and close jump rings. Grasp the ring on each side of the opening with pliers (Figure 3).

5. Gently push one side away from you while pulling the other side toward you, so the ring opens from side to side (Figure 4). To close, reverse the directions of your hands.

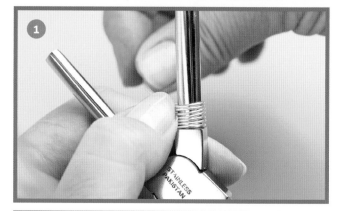

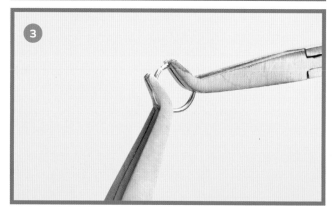

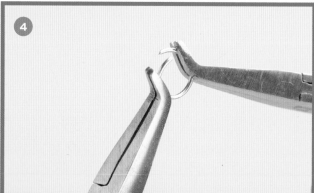

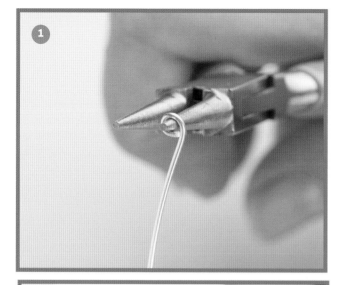

BASIC EAR WIRES

1. Make a small loop on the end of 1½" (3.8 cm) of wire (Figure 1).

2. Hold the loop against a Sharpie marker and bend the wire over the marker away from the loop (Figure 2).

3. Use round-nose pliers to make a small bend up at the end of the wire (Figure 3). Use a cup bur or file to smooth the end of the wire. Repeat for the other ear wire.

Tip: It is best to make ear wires with 20-gauge full-hard wire because the wire holds its shape. Thinner wire can sometimes be too weak, and a thicker gauge can be hard on the ears. Use sterling silver, Argentium, or niobium wire to avoid potential sensitivity if you are allergic to certain metals.

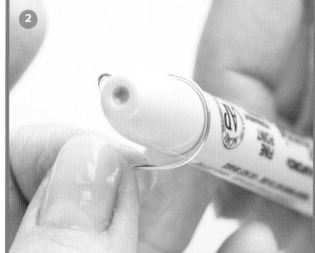

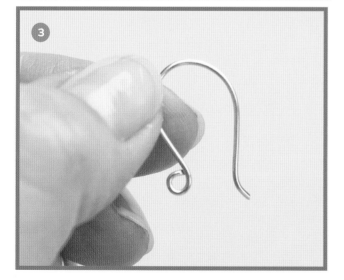

Chapter 6

Cold Connections

Lots of jewelry can be made, and pieces connected, without ever needing a torch and solder. Every project in this book uses a cold connection of some sort, and it can be anything from connecting a bead with a wrapped loop to riveting two pieces of sheet together.

We use a variety of easy cold-connection techniques within the projects. The simplest is using a micro screw and nut, but all of the riveting techniques are simple with the right tools. We've chosen to use prefabricated rivets, so half the job is done for you already!

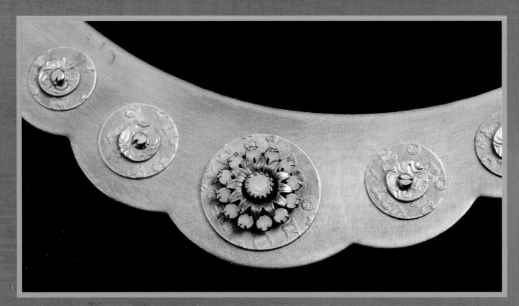

↖ *Camelot, see page 126*

↘ Center punches

Riveting Tools + Techniques

The simplest rivets are formed using manufactured nail-head rivets or tube rivets and eyelets. You can find them at hardware stores and jewelry suppliers. Snap rivets are also available as a specialty item from jewelry suppliers. They come with male and female sides that snap together with the use of a snap rivet tool.

RIVETING HAMMER
This hammer has one flat face and one chiseled face. It is primarily used for making wire into rivets. The round face can also be used for gently folding over tube rivets.

SNAP RIVET TOOL
Specifically made for use with snap rivets to compress the two pieces together. Use this tool with a nylon hammer only.

CENTER PUNCHES
These tools are used to flare the tube rivet or eyelet and begin the process of folding the edges over.

↗ Snap rivet tool

↘ Nail-head rivets

↘ Riveting hammer

↘ Tube rivets

↘ Snap rivets

Riveting with a nail-head rivet

1. Using metal hole-punch pliers, make a hole in the pieces of metal to be connected. Choose the hole-punch pliers with a hole size that matches the diameter of your nail. The nail should fit as snugly as possible into the holes. File the back of the holes flat to remove any burrs.

2. Insert the nail into the holes. Trim the nail end to ¹⁄₁₆" (2 mm) with heavy-duty flush cutters (Figure 1).

3. Place the nail, head side down, on the bench block. Using the chisel end of the riveting hammer, tap gently around the perimeter of the cut nail to begin flaring the edges (Figure 2).

4. Once the edges have flared slightly, use the other side of the riveting hammer to flatten the rivet (Figure 3).

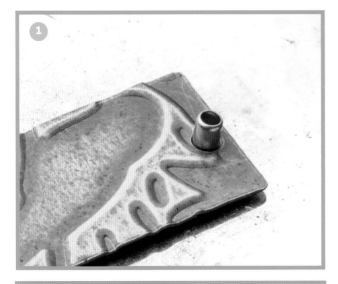

Riveting with a tube rivet + eyelet

1. Using metal hole-punch pliers, make a hole in the pieces of metal to be connected. Choose the hole-punch pliers with a hole size that matches the diameter of your tube rivet/eyelet and make sure the length of your rivets is about 1 mm longer than the thickness of your pieces of metal. The tube rivet/eyelet should fit as snugly as possible into the holes. File the back of the holes flat to remove any burrs.

2. Insert the tube rivet/eyelet into the holes. Turn the piece upside down on a rubber bench block with the tube side up (Figure 1).

3. Place the center punch or eyelet tool inside the tube and hammer gently to begin to flare the tube (Figure 2).

4. Use the ball end of a chasing hammer to continue flaring the tube (Figure 3).

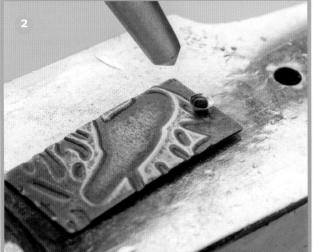

Riveting with a snap rivet

1. Using metal hole-punch pliers, make a hole in the pieces of metal to be connected. Choose the hole-punch pliers with a hole size that matches the diameter of your snap rivet. The snap rivet should fit as snugly as possible into the holes. Insert the top rivet through the holes and snap the back rivet into place (Figure 1).

2. Turn the piece upside down on a steel bench block. If the snap rivet has a stone on the front, place a few Pro-Polish pads between the stone and the bench block before hammering (Figure 2).

3. Place the snap riveting tool on the back of the rivet and, using a plastic hammer, rotate the riveting tool in a circular motion while hammering (Figure 3).

Micro Screws + Nuts

Jewelry suppliers and hobby stores sell tiny screws with matching nuts that can be used almost anywhere a rivet can. The end of the screw can be flared like a rivet or, alternatively, the screw and nut can simply be tightened and secured with a drop of superglue. They come in a variety of diameters and lengths.

MICRO SCREWDRIVER

This small screwdriver is commonly found at drugstores and used for eyeglass repair. It is a useful tool to tighten micro screws for jewelry making.

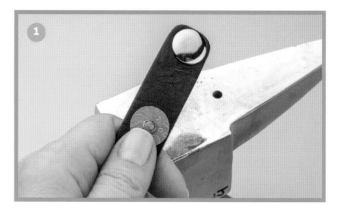

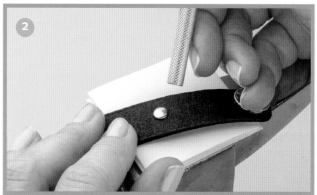

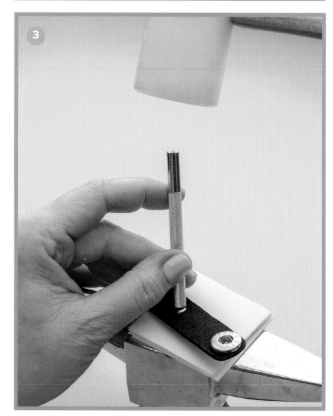

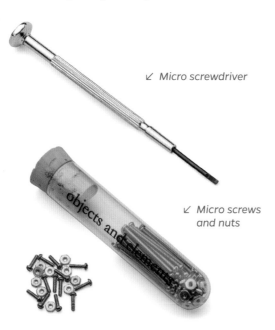

↙ *Micro screwdriver*

↙ *Micro screws and nuts*

To use a micro screw + nut

1. Using metal hole-punch pliers, make a hole in the pieces of metal to be connected. Choose the hole-punch pliers with a hole size that matches the diameter of your screw. The screw should fit as snugly as possible into the holes. File the back of the holes flat to remove any burrs.

2. Insert the screw into the holes and attach the nut to the screw. Tighten the screw and nut with a micro screwdriver and flat- or chain-nose pliers.

3. Using heavy-duty flush cutters, trim the end of the screw to 1/16" (2 mm). Turn the piece upside down and rivet the end (see Steps 3 and 4 of Riveting with a Nail-Head Rivet) (Figure 1).

Optional: Alternatively, trim the screw flush with the nut, file the end, and apply a drop of superglue.

GLUE

Glue is also considered a cold connection. In this book, we used E6000, which is an industrial-strength permanent-bonding adhesive; Bead Fix, which is a cyanoacrylate glue; and Mod Podge, which is an all-in-one glue, sealer, and finish.

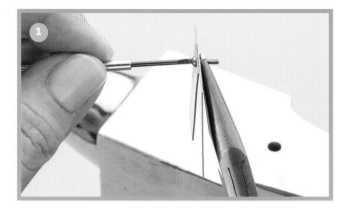

↙ E6000, Bead Fix, and Mod Podge

Other Useful Tools for Cold Connections

Chain-nose pliers (see page 33)

Flat-nose pliers (see page 33)

Metal hole-punch pliers (see 16)

Heavy-duty flush cutters (see page 15)

Chasing hammer (see page 27)

Steel bench block (see page 27)

Anvil (see page 36)

Rubber bench block (see page 36)

File (see page 53)

Leather sandbag (see page 27)

Chapter 7

Patina + Color

Patina refers to the changing colors that occur naturally or intentionally on the surface of metal. We've primarily used liver of sulfur to patina the projects in this book, and a few use heat patina. Two other easy methods we used to color metal are nail polish and spray paint.

There are many options you can explore to enhance the color of your metal, including alcohol inks, enamels, colored pencils, hobby paints, and more. For further reading, see the Bibliography on page 142.

See Chapter 8, Finishing (page 52), for methods of sealing and protecting your patina or color.

↖ *Inner Vision, see page 72*

↘ *Liver of sulfur*

Patina + Coloring Tools

LIVER OF SULFUR

Liver of sulfur is a chemical traditionally used to darken silver, although it also works on copper and bronze. It comes in a liquid, gel, or solid chunk form and has a strong odor. Liver of sulfur can produce an array of colors on various metals from blues and magentas to black. Many artists have discovered various techniques for drawing out a rainbow of colors. For further reading, see the Bibliography on page 142.

To add patina using liver of sulfur

Clean your jewelry thoroughly and dry it before applying patina. Work in a well-ventilated area. The temperature of the water, the length of time you leave it in, the age of the liver of sulfur, and the type of metal you're using all affect the color you get from the solution. You can get beautiful blues, pinks, and purples, along with the usual black.

1. Prepare a solution with liquid, lump, or gel liver of sulfur following the manufacturer's directions. Dip your piece into the solution (Figures 1 and 2).

Tip: Dipping, rinsing, and redipping will give you the greatest control over the color changes.

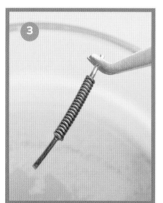

2. Remove the piece when it reaches the desired color (Figure 3). Rinse and dry.

3. Polish lightly with a Pro-Polish pad or 0000 steel wool to remove some of the patina (Figure 4), but leave the dark color in the recesses of the piece (Figure 5).

It is important to remove any residual oils or fingerprints so the patina or paint will adhere to the surface of the metal. There are many methods for cleaning the metal prior to these applications: you can use steel wool, sandpaper, Bar Keepers Friend powder and a green scrub pad, or soap and water.

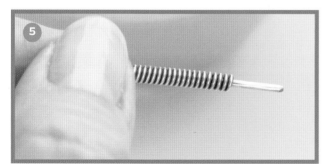

BUTANE MICRO TORCH

To patina using heat + flame

Fire will change the color of certain metals. Copper, in particular, will often take on beautiful shades of red when heated with a torch, and bronze turns a warm chocolate color. Some artists recommend cleaning the metal with an abrasive powder and green scrub pad before applying heat patina; others simply sand the metal or use steel wool to clean the metal surface. And some artists recommend quenching the metal (see page 21) to get the best color, while others claim air-drying gets the best color. We recommend experimenting to find your favorite method. For further reading, see the Bibliography on page 142.

1. See Safety First! on page 20 before you begin. Place your metal on a heatproof surface.

2. Move the flame back and forth over the metal for a few seconds, then remove the flame and check the color. It may continue to turn color even after the flame is removed. Continue this process until you achieve a color you like. Quench or air cool (Figures 1 and 2).

3. Apply a protective finish (see Finishing, page 52) to preserve the patina.

OVEN PATINA

1. Preheat the oven to 300°F (149°C).

2. Place your clean copper components on a cookie sheet. Bake for about 17 minutes, checking frequently after 10 minutes, until you reach the desired patina (Figure 1. "Before" disc on the left and "After" disc on the right). Quench or air cool.

3. Apply a protective finish to preserve the patina.

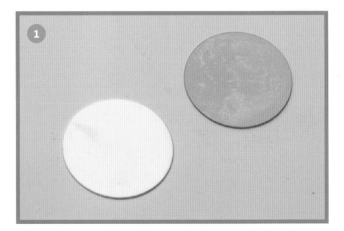

↖ *Nail polish*

↖ *Gilders Paste*

NAIL POLISH + SPRAY PAINT

Nail polish is an easy and economical way to provide an enamel-like coating to metal. There are a range of options from translucent to opaque and matte to glossy.

Spray paint is another easy way to add color to metal and also comes in a variety of finishes.

To color with nail polish + spray paint:
Always work in a well-ventilated area when using products that produce fumes.

1. Clean the surface of your metal and sand lightly to create a tooth.

2. Paint the metal and let dry; repeat if necessary.

3. Apply a protective finish over the spray paint application. This is not necessary for nail polish.

GILDERS PASTE

Gilders Paste is a topical colorant used on metal for a surface effect. It comes in a variety of colors that transfer directly to the metal.

To use Gilders Paste
1. Apply the paste to metal with your fingers or a soft cloth. Let dry. Reapply if needed until you reach the desired color.

2. Buff with a soft cloth.

Other Useful Tools for Patina + Color

Utility pliers (see page 21)

Soldering blocks (see page 20)

Annealing pan with pumice (see page 21)

Quenching bowl (see page 21)

Bar Keepers Friend powder (see page 54)

Scotch-Brite green scrub pad (see page 54)

Sandpaper (see page 31)

0000 steel wool (see page 54)

Polishing cloth/pad (see page 54)

Protective spray finish (see page 55)

Renaissance Wax (see page 55)

Chapter 8

Finishing

Finishing your jewelry professionally makes all the difference. There are many different ways to finish your jewelry, from sandpaper to tumble polishing. You'll choose a method depending upon what kind of finish you want on your metal. Sandpaper leaves a brushed finish, tumbling leaves a high shine, and waxes and protective sprays come in both matte and glossy. Follow the manufacturer's instructions for the waxes and protective sprays.

Be sure to clean your work before applying color or patina, sand rough edges to eliminate burrs, smooth the back of punched holes, and pinch in the tails of your wirework. Every detail of finishing is important.

↘ Hand files

IMPORTANT:
To protect yourself from inhaling metal dust or getting particles in your eyes, always use a dust or respiratory mask and protective eyewear when filing, sanding metal, or using steel wool. Use gloves when handling sharp metal.

Finishing Tools

HAND FILES

Jeweler's files come in a variety of sizes, shapes, and cuts (coarseness). The lower the cut number, the coarser the file; a #2 file is considered a good general file. It's also good to have a set of needle files for small pieces. Match the shape of the file to the contour of the piece you're working on.

To use a hand file

The teeth of all metal files are made to cut only in one direction; they should not be used like fingernail files with a back-and-forth motion.

Place the file against your metal and push the file away from you. For every stroke, pick up the file again, place it back on the metal, and push it away.

SALON BOARD

The 100/180 coarse-grit salon boards used in the manicure industry are perfect for filing the sharp edges off metal and wire. They come in various grits, are easy to find, and are inexpensive.

SANDPAPER

Sandpaper comes in a variety of grits for final finishing, including sanding off sharp burrs and fine smoothing. The smaller the number grit, the coarser the sandpaper. Sanding is used for different purposes: for creating tooth to prepare the surface for another application, for texturing to create a matte finish, or for polishing to create a smooth finish.

SANDING SPONGES

Sanding sponges look like chalkboard erasers, but they are covered in sandpaper. They have a larger area of sandpaper than nail files and are good for larger jobs such as roughing up sheet metal to take paints and inks better. They come in various grits and can be found at hardware stores.

↘ Salon boards

↖ Sandpaper

↘ Sanding sponges

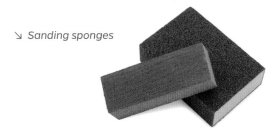

STEEL WOOL

Superfine 0000 steel wool is great for cleaning your metal before working with it. It can simultaneously clean, straighten, and polish. It also can be used for removing liver of sulfur oxidation prior to final tumbling. Always dry your metal after cleaning, pickling, and rinsing and using patinas and rinsing; moisture can cause steel to rust. Using steel wool on wet metal may trap small particles of steel wool in the metalwork, and an unexpected rust "patina" can form. Be sure to rinse your pieces before you continue to work with them, as steel wool creates metal dust.

SCOTCH-BRITE PAD + BAR KEEPERS FRIEND CLEANING + POLISHING POWDER

Using these tools together will clean the surface of your metal thoroughly. Remember, these are abrasives and will scratch the surface of the metal. Use a circular motion to provide a more consistent finish.

ROTARY TUMBLER + MIXED STAINLESS STEEL SHOT

Often associated with rock tumbling, this same electrical piece of equipment can be used to polish wire and metal jewelry. The barrel must be filled with a tumbling medium such as mixed stainless steel shot (available from a jeweler's supplier), water, and a bit of burnishing compound or non-ultra liquid dish detergent. The tumbling action against the shot polishes the metal or wire to a high shine. The tumbling action also helps work-harden, or stiffen, the wire.

Used in jewelry tumblers for final high shine, stainless steel shot comes in several shapes. The weight of stainless steel, combined with the mixed shapes, makes it a good choice for polishing uniformly on complex shapes. A standard rotary tumbler uses 2 pounds of mixed stainless steel shot.

To tumble polish

Before tumbling, clean your oxidized jewelry with a polishing cloth or fine steel wool to remove some of the blackening agent. Otherwise, the tumbling will just shine the blackened color into a gunmetal appearance rather than an antiqued appearance with polished highlights.

1. Place 1 to 2 pounds of mixed-shaped stainless steel shot in the barrel of the tumbler.

↘ *From left: Steel wool, Bar Keepers Friend, Scotch-Brite pad*

↗ *Rotary tumbler and mixed stainless steel shot*

↙ *Burnishing compound*

↖ *Polishing cloths*

2. Add enough water to cover the shot plus 1" (2.5 cm), a pinch of liquid dish detergent (non-ultra) or burnishing compound, and your piece of jewelry. Seal the barrel and tumble for 1 to 2 hours.

3. Drain the water through a fine-mesh sieve and remove your pieces. Rinse the jewelry and the shot with clear water. Dry the jewelry.

4. Spread the shot out on a dish towel to dry; never put it away wet.

BURNISHING COMPOUND

This special formulation is added to tumblers to keep the tumbling solution clean and produce the finest shine on metal.

POLISHING CLOTH/PAD

Jewelry polishing cloths are infused with a polishing compound and can be used for cleaning metal and eliminating tarnish. Pro-Polish pads are another option.

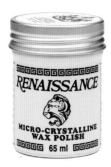

↗ *Renaissance Wax*

Sealants

RENAISSANCE WAX

Renaissance Wax was first used to preserve artifacts in the British Museum. Jewelers use this wax to protect their jewelry from tarnish and corrosion.

PROTECTIVE SPRAY FINISH

A nonyellowing spray finish in matte or glossy helps to seal the color of the patina.

ANTI-TARNISH STRIPS

Moisture is a culprit in tarnishing silver. Store your sterling wire and jewelry in an airtight container with anti-tarnish strips or a packet of silica desiccant (such as the little packages found in purses, shoes, and suitcases).

↗ *Protective spray finish, anti-tarnish strips*

Spinner

Kristi Evenson

Tools

+ Texture hammers (optional)
+ Chasing hammer
+ Steel bench block
+ Metal file
+ 220-grit sandpaper
+ Letter stamping set, ⅛" (3 mm) or smaller
+ Ball-peen hammer
+ Fine-point Sharpie marker
+ Ruler
+ 1.8 mm metal hole-punch pliers
+ Chain- or flat-nose pliers
+ Round-nose pliers
+ Liver of sulfur
+ 0000 steel wool

Materials

+ 1 brass 1¼" (3.2 cm) 22-gauge disc
+ 1 copper 1" (2.5 cm) 22-gauge disc
+ 1 sterling ½" (1.3 cm) 22-gauge disc
+ 1 copper ¼" (6 mm) 22-gauge disc
+ 8" (20.5 cm) of sterling 18-gauge wire
+ 22" (56 cm) of copper 2mm ball chain necklace

Finished length

+ Pendant: 2" (5 cm)
+ Necklace: 22" (56 cm)

1. Use either texture hammers or the rounded end of the chasing hammer to create textures on the brass, sterling, and small ¼" (6 mm) copper discs. Turn the pieces over after texturing them, and lightly hammer the backs of the discs so that they lie flat. File and sand the edges smooth.

2. Texture the 1" (2.5 cm) copper disc lightly with the rounded end of the chasing hammer. Stamp a favorite phrase around the outer edge with the alphabet stamps and ball-peen hammer. Make sure to do a test run on a piece of scrap metal to make sure the phrase will fit around the disc. Once this disc is stamped, turn it over and lightly hammer the back with the chasing hammer so it lies flat.

3. Mark the center of the ¼" (6 mm) copper disc with the Sharpie and make a hole at the mark with the hole-punch pliers.

4. Center the ¼" (6 mm) copper disc on top of the sterling disc and make a mark through the hole with the Sharpie onto the sterling disc. Make a hole at the mark using the hole-punch pliers. Repeat for the large copper disc and brass disc. Turn each of the discs over one at a time and gently strike the punched hole to flatten the pieces again.

5. Place the 8" (20.5 cm) length of sterling wire on the bench block and hammer about 2" (5 cm) on one end with the chasing hammer to slightly flatten it.

6. With chain- or flat-nose pliers, grasp the wire at the 2" (5 cm) point where you flattened it, and make a 90° bend in the wire. Holding that bend with your fingers, slide the discs onto the longer end of the wire, starting with the smallest copper disc, and working toward the largest disc, all facing the bend in the wire.

7. Place the chain-nose pliers up against the back of the brass disc and make another 90° in the long end of the wire. Begin a wrapped loop about ¾" (2 cm) from the edge of the brass disc. Wrap the loop multiple times, trim the wire, and pinch in the end with chain-nose pliers.

8. Oxidize the pendant and chain with liver of sulfur; rinse and dry. Remove the excess patina with fine steel wool. Rinse and dry.

Resources

Discs, stamping set: beaducation.com.

Metal Petals

Jane Dickerson

Tools

+ Fine-point Sharpie marker
+ Ruler
+ Power Punch pliers
+ 100/180 coarse salon board
+ Do It Best flat black all-purpose interior/exterior fast-drying spray paint
+ Krylon Matte Finish 1311 spray
+ Disc cutter
+ Spiral metal stamp
+ Ball-peen hammer
+ Steel bench block
+ 1.8 mm metal hole-punch pliers
+ Eyeglass repair mini screwdriver
+ Flat- or chain-nose pliers
+ Heavy-duty flush cutters
+ Riveting hammer
+ Superglue

Finished length

+ One size

Materials

+ One 1½" (3.8 cm) wide smooth raw brass cuff
+ One 13mm deep pie-crust bezel in brass ox
+ One 2⅛" (5.4 cm) brass filigree 5-petal flower
+ 24-gauge brass sheet
+ 1 brass ¹⁄₁₆" (2 mm) shank diameter × ⁹⁄₃₂" (7.1 mm) long micro screw
+ 1 brass 4mm micro nut

3. Using the disc cutter, cut a ¾" (2 cm) disc from the brass sheet. Place the disc on the steel bench block and texture one side with the spiral metal stamp and ball-peen hammer.

4. Punch a hole in the middle of the textured disc and the 13mm pie-pan bezel with the 1.8 mm metal hole-punch pliers. Punch a hole in the middle of the filigree flower with the Power Punch pliers ³⁄₃₂" (2.4 mm) punch.

5. Insert a micro screw through the front of the pie-crust bezel, the textured disc, the flower, and the brass cuff. Thread a nut onto the back of the screw. Tighten the screw and nut with the mini screwdriver and chain- or flat-nose pliers.

6. Snip the back of the screw to about ¹⁄₁₆" (2 mm) above the nut with heavy-duty flush cutters. Place the bracelet upside down on the steel bench block. Use the chisel side of the riveting hammer to gently flare the screw, then use the flat side of the hammer to flatten it (as with a nail-head rivet; see page 44). Alternatively, cut the screw flush with the nut, file smooth, and add a drop of superglue to the back of the screw/nut.

Resources

Brass cuff, pie-crust bezel: bsueboutiques.com. Brass filigree flower: theartfloozy.etsy.com; kabeladesign.com. Brass micro screws and nuts 200, 1.8 mm metal hole punch pliers: objectsandelements.com. Eyeglass repair mini screwdriver: drugstore. Tools: riogrande.com. Pepetools disc cutter, Power Punch pliers, brass sheet, spiral metal stamp: beaducation.com. Flat black spray paint: doitbest.com. Spray matte finish: michaels.com.

1. Mark the center of the front of the brass cuff with the Sharpie. Make a hole at that mark with the Power Punch pliers using the ³⁄₃₂" (2.4 mm) punch. File the back of the hole with the nail file to remove the rough edges.

2. Scuff the front of the filigree flower with the salon board, rinse, and dry. Spray the flower with the black flat paint and let dry; repeat. When the paint is dry, follow with a coat or two of the matte finish spray; let dry.

Shadow

Jane Dickerson

Tools

+ Texture hammer
+ Steel bench block
+ Liver of sulfur
+ Krylon Matte Finish 1311 spray
+ Pro-Polish pad
+ Renaissance Wax
+ Soft cloth
+ 1.8 mm metal hole-punch pliers
+ Eyeglass repair mini screwdriver
+ Flat- or chain-nose pliers
+ Heavy-duty flush cutter
+ 100/180 coarse salon board
+ Superglue

Finished length

+ 1¼" (3.2 cm) including the ear wire

Materials

+ 2 sterling silver ¾" (2 cm) 22-gauge discs
+ 2 rosy copper 10×5mm bead caps
+ 2 brass ¹⁄₁₆" (2 mm) shank diameter × ⁹⁄₃₂" (7.1 mm) long micro screws
+ 2 brass 4mm micro nuts
+ 1 pair of ear wires

1. Place the discs on the steel bench block and texture the front with a texture hammer.

2. Clean the discs and bead caps with soap and water and dry. Oxidize the discs in liver of sulfur; rinse and dry. Oxidize the bead caps until they turn matte black; rinse and dry. Spray the bead caps with the matte finish spray. Clean and polish the silver discs with a Pro-Polish pad to remove the excess patina. Seal the patina on the silver discs with Renaissance Wax.

3. Make a hole in the top and in the center of each disc with the 1.8 mm hole-punch pliers.

4. Insert a micro screw through the hole in the front of a bead cap and the center hole on the front of a silver disc. Screw a nut onto the screw. Tighten the screw and nut with the mini screwdriver and flat- or chain-nose pliers. Trim the screw so it is flush with the nut and file smooth. Place a drop of superglue on the screw and nut. Repeat for the other earring.

5. Attach an ear wire to the top hole of each disc.

Resources

Sterling silver discs: metalliferous.com. Bead caps: bsueboutiques.com. Texture hammer (interchangeable nine-face hammer): beaducation.com. Micro screws and nuts: objectsandelements.com. Eyeglass mini screwdriver: drugstore. Ear wire, spray matte finish: michaels .com. Renaissance Wax: objectsandelements.com.

Pink Petals

Denise Peck

Materials

+ 24-gauge pink aluminum sheet
+ 36-gauge textured copper sheet
+ 5" (12.5 cm) of 20-gauge sterling wire

Tools

+ Disc cutter
+ 1.5 mm metal hole-punch pliers
+ Mandrel or pencil
+ Flush cutters
+ Round-nose pliers
+ Ruler
+ Fine-point Sharpie marker
+ Metal file

Finished length

+ 1¾" (4.5 cm)

1. Cut two 1" (2.5 cm) aluminum discs with the disc cutter.

2. Cut two ¾" (2 cm) copper discs with the disc cutter.

3. Mark the center on each of the 4 discs with the Sharpie and, using the hole-punch pliers, make a hole on the marks.

4. Gently fold 1 disc around the pencil or mandrel to form a U shape. Repeat for the other 3 discs.

5. Flush cut the wire in half. Using round-nose pliers, make a small simple loop on one end of each wire, forming an eye pin.

6. Thread the pink disc and copper disc onto the eye pin. Repeat for the second earring.

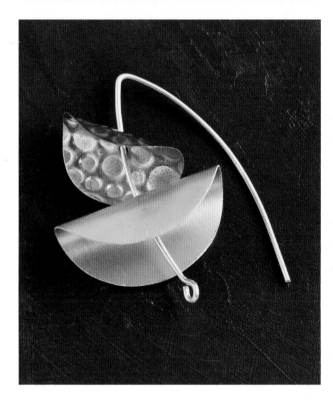

7. Use the Sharpie to make a mark on the eye pin 1¾" (4.5 cm) from the top disc. Bend the wire over the tip of the round-nose pliers at the mark to form the ear wire. Repeat for the other earring. File the end of both ear wires smooth.

Resources

Pink aluminum sheet: eastwestdye.com. Copper textured sheet: lillypillydesigns.com.

Ring Around the Rosy

Jane Dickerson

Materials

+ 1 sterling silver rivetable ring blank
+ 1 lime enamel 23.2mm (large) disc
+ 1 violet enamel 18.3mm (medium) disc
+ 1 mandarin enamel 14mm (small) disc
+ 1 pale green patinated 8mm flower bead cap

Tools

+ Painter's tape
+ Scissors
+ Round needle file
+ Chasing hammer
+ Steel bench block
+ Metal ring mandrel
+ Leather sandbag
+ Heavy-duty flush cutters

Finished size

+ Varies

1. Stack the large, medium, and small enamel discs on the pin of the ring. If they wobble a lot, remove them and wrap a small strip of painter's tape around the pin and place the discs back on the pin. Make sure the tape is not showing. It doesn't need to be a snug fit; just eliminate the excess wobble.

2. Using a round needle file, ream out the center of the bead cap until is just fits over the pin of the ring. Take your time and do not make this hole too big; it should be a close fit. Remove the bead cap from the pin and turn it upside down on the steel bench block. Gently tap the back of the bead cap with the chasing hammer to open the petals.

3. Slip the bead cap back onto the pin and place the ring securely on the ring mandrel. Place the ring mandrel on the leather sandbag. Using heavy-duty flush cutters, trim the pin until it is about $\frac{1}{16}$" (2 mm) above the base of the bead cap.

4. With the ball side of the chasing hammer, gently tap the pin to flair it out and secure the components. Be careful not to hammer the enamel pieces, focus on the pin. When riveted properly, the discs and bead cap will be compressed and the ring will be secure.

Resources

Rivetable ring blank: beaducation.com. Enamel discs: objectsandelements.com. Bead cap: patinaqueen.etsy.com. Tools: riogrande.com. Painter's tape: doitbest.com.

Ring Around the Rosy

Blue Moon

Jane Dickerson

Materials

+ 24-gauge copper sheet or a 1"
  (2.5 cm) copper disc and a ¼"
  (6 mm) copper disc

+ 3 gunmetal 5mm 21-gauge
  jump rings

+ 18" (45.5 cm) of black 5mm
  round chain

+ 1 gunmetal 14.5mm lobster clasp

Tools

+ Disc cutter
+ Bar Keepers Friend powder
+ Scotch-Brite green scrub pad
+ Liver of sulfur
+ 1.8 mm metal hole-punch pliers
+ Fine-point Sharpie marker
+ 100/180 coarse salon board
+ Essie Coat Azure nail polish
+ Sheet of paper
+ Center punch
+ Ball-peen hammer
+ Steel bench block

Finished length

+ 18" (45.5 cm)

1. Punch a 1" (2.5 cm) copper disc and a ¼" (6 mm) copper disc from the sheet metal (or use precut discs).

2. Clean both pieces with Bar Keepers Friend, water, and a green scrub pad, working in a circular motion. Rinse and dry. Oxidize both pieces with liver of sulfur until black. Rinse and dry.

3. Using the hole-punch pliers, make a hole in the center of the small disc. Line up the top of the small disc with the top of the large disc and mark through the hole with a Sharpie. Punch a hole at the mark.

4. Use the salon board to remove the rough edges on the back of the discs where the hole was punched. Rinse and dry both pieces.

5. Place the discs, front side up, on a piece of paper. Paint half of the large disc and the entire small disc with the nail polish; let dry. Repeat for a second coat.

6. When the nail polish is completely dry, use a center punch and ball-peen hammer to hammer small dots in the polish on the large disc, revealing the black underneath.

7. Use a jump ring to attach the small disc to the front of the large disc. Attach a chain and the lobster clasp with the remaining jump rings.

Resources

Copper sheet, liver of sulfur: riogrande.com. Black chain: chaingallery.com, michaels.com. Jump rings, lobster clasp: ornamentea.com. Nail polish: bedbathandbeyond .com. Bar Keepers Friend powder: doitbest.com. Pepetools disc cutter, copper discs (optional): beaducation.com. 1.8 mm metal hole-punch pliers: objectsandelements.com.

Heaven's Gate

Denise Peck

Materials

+ One 30 x 50 mm Vintaj natural brass tag
+ 10 brass 6mm jump rings
+ 10 Czech glass 5mm rondelles
+ 6" (15 cm) of 18-gauge brass wire
+ 36" (91.5 cm) of hand-dyed shibori ribbon

Tools

+ Deco Etch Paisley Swirl die
+ Vintaj Sizzix BIGkick machine
+ Vintaj Reliefing Block
+ Ruler
+ Fine-point Sharpie marker
+ 1.5 mm metal hole-punch pliers
+ 2 pairs of chain-nose pliers
+ 12 mm mandrel

Finished length

+ Varies

If you don't have a BIGkick machine, you can texture the brass tag with coins or textured sheet (see page 29) and proceed to Step 2.

1. Imprint the brass tag with the Deco Etch Paisley Swirl die using the BIGkick Sizzix machine, following the manufacturer's instructions. Sand both sides with the Reliefing Block.

2. Using a ruler and Sharpie, make five marks down each side of the tag, equidistant from each other, and 2 mm in from the edge. Make holes at the marks with the hole-punch pliers.

3. String a bead onto each jump ring and then thread a jump ring through each of the holes along the sides of the tag. Use two chain-nose pliers to close each jump ring after it's added.

4. Coil the brass wire around the 12 mm mandrel to make a coil 3 loops long. Remove the coil from the mandrel and thread it onto the top hole of the tag. Spread the 3 coils out from each other gently with your fingers and string the ribbon through the coil.

Resources

Sizzix BIGkick, Deco Etch Paisley Swirl die, and brass tag: vintaj.com. Shibori ribbon: fibergoddess.net.

Sunday Afternoon

Denise Peck

Materials

+ 6" (15 cm) of sterling ¼" (6 mm) flat wire
+ 4" (10 cm) of sterling 20-gauge half-hard wire
+ 6 sterling 6mm jump rings
+ 15×25mm Czech glass bead
+ 1 sterling 15mm lobster clasp

Tools

+ Metal shears
+ Ball-peen hammer
+ Steel bench block
+ Metal file
+ Bracelet mandrel
+ 1.5 mm metal hole-punch pliers
+ Liver of sulfur
+ 0000 steel wool
+ 2 pairs of chain-nose pliers
+ Round-nose pliers
+ Flush cutters
+ Rotary tumbler
+ Mixed stainless steel shot

Finished size

+ 7" (18 cm)

1. Cut the flat wire in half using metal shears. Hammer both ends of both pieces with the flat side of the ball-peen hammer to form a paddle on each end. File the edges smooth. Texture both pieces with the ball end of the ball-peen hammer.

2. Gently curve both pieces around the bracelet mandrel. Make a centered hole on all four ends, about 3 mm from the edge using the hole-punch pliers.

3. Oxidize the pieces with liver of sulfur (see page 49), rinse, and dry. Clean with steel wool to remove the excess oxidation. Tumble for 30 minutes to 1 hour to polish and work-harden.

4. Center the bead on the 20-gauge wire and begin a wire-wrapped loop on each end. Before closing the loop, thread one bracelet piece onto each loop; finish the wrapped loops. Trim the wires and pinch in the ends with chain-nose pliers.

5. Connect 5 jump rings in a chain and attach one end to one side of the bracelet. Attach a single jump ring to the lobster clasp on the other end.

Resources

Flat silver wire: riogrande.com. Czech glass bead: cascadiabeads.etsy.com.

Inner Vision

Jane Dickerson

Materials

+ 24-gauge copper sheet
+ 32-gauge tin sheet
+ 6" (15 cm) of 18-gauge copper wire
+ 1 pair of ear wires

Tools

+ Disc cutter
+ Ruler
+ Fine-point Sharpie marker
+ Metal shears
+ Nylon or rawhide hammer
+ Steel bench block
+ Alcohol wipes
+ 100/180 coarse salon board
+ 1.5 mm metal hole-punch pliers
+ Power Punch pliers
+ Spiral metal stamp
+ Ball-peen hammer
+ Bar Keepers Friend powder
+ Scotch-Brite green scrub pad
+ Fireproof work surface (cookie sheet)
+ Oven
+ Krylon Matte Finish 1311 spray or Renaissance Wax
+ Soft cloth
+ Maybelline #320 (Green with Envy) Color Show nail polish
+ Round-nose pliers
+ Stepped forming pliers (2–9 mm)
+ Flush cutters

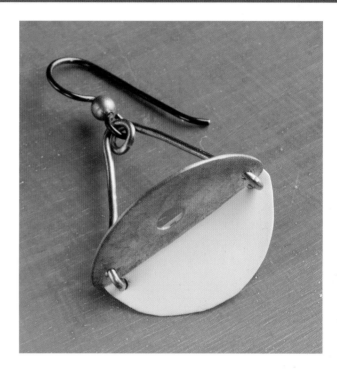

Finished length

+ 1¾" (4.5 cm) including the ear wire

1. Using the disc cutter, cut 1" (2.5 cm) discs from the copper sheet and the tin sheet.

2. Draw a line across the center of each disc with the ruler and Sharpie. Cut the discs in half with shears and snip off the points of the sharp corners. Gently flatten the discs on the steel bench block with the nylon mallet if they are distorted by the cutting. File the edges and round the corners with the salon board. Remove the Sharpie line with an alcohol wipe if necessary.

3. Make a hole in each corner of the copper pieces with the 1.5 mm hole-punch pliers. Using the Power Punch pliers, punch a $^5/_{32}$" (4 mm) hole in the center of each copper piece. Line up one copper piece over a tin piece and mark through the 1.5 mm holes with the Sharpie, making a dot on the tin sheet beneath. Punch 1.5 mm holes in the tin sheet at the marks; repeat for the other tin sheet. File the back of all of the pieces to remove the rough edges from the punched holes.

4. Place the copper pieces on the steel bench block, front side up. Using a ball-peen hammer and steel bench block, texture the front of the pieces with the spiral metal stamp.

5. To color the copper, preheat the oven to 300°F (149°C). Clean the copper pieces with Bar Keepers Friend powder, water, and a green scrub pad, working in a circular motion. Rinse and dry. Place the copper pieces, front side up, on a cookie sheet and bake for about 17 minutes. Check them after 10 minutes and frequently thereafter. Once you see the color change to a tropical orange, remove the pieces and let them air cool. Transfer the cooled copper pieces to a sheet of paper and spray with Krylon Matte Finish or seal with Renaissance Wax.

6. Paint the front of the tin pieces with nail polish and let dry; repeat.

7. Place the copper pieces over the tin pieces and make sure the edges line up. If necessary, trim the tin pieces with shears.

8. Cut two 3" (7.5 cm) pieces of 18-gauge copper wire. Place the center of one wire over the smallest (2 mm) jaw of the stepped forming pliers and wrap both sides of the wire completely around the jaw, making a loop in the center (Figure 1).

9. Bring the ends of the wires together and flush cut them so they are even.

10. Using the next step up on the pliers (3 mm), make a simple loop on each end of the wire, both going in the same direction and perpendicular to the center loop (Figure 2). Repeat with the other 3" (7.5 cm) piece of wire.

11. Using chain-nose pliers, open the end loops as you would a jump ring and attach the copper sheet, front first, and then the tin sheet, front first. Close the loops. Attach an ear wire to the center loop. Repeat for the other earring.

Resources

K&S Create with Metal tin sheet, Bar Keepers Friend powder: doitbest.com. Pepetools disc cutter, scissor shears, spiral metal stamp, Power Punch pliers, 1.5 mm hole-punch pliers, multistep pliers: beaducation.com. Nail polish: bedbathandbeyond.com. Copper sheet, copper wire: riogrande.com. Ear wires, spray matte finish: michaels.com. Renaissance Wax: objectsandelements.com.

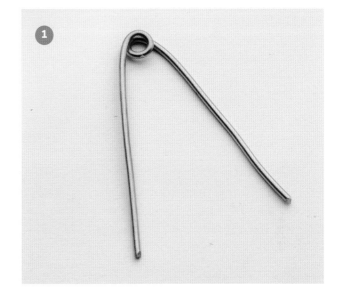

Eco Revival
Jane Dickerson

+ 3' (91.4 cm) of 2 mm cording
+ One ¹⁄₁₆" (2 mm) shank diameter × ⁹⁄₃₂" (7.1 mm) long brass micro screw
+ One 4mm brass micro nut

Tools

+ 1.8 mm metal hole-punch pliers
+ Fine-point Sharpie marker
+ 100/180 coarse-grit salon board
+ Spiral metal stamp
+ Brass mallet or ball-peen hammer
+ Steel bench block
+ African Bronze Gilders Paste
+ Soft cloth
+ Disc cutter
+ Metal shears
+ Dapping block
+ Eyeglass mini screwdriver
+ Flat- or chain-nose pliers
+ Heavy-duty flush cutters
+ Scissors
+ Superglue

Materials

+ 1⁵⁄₈" × 2³⁄₃₂" (4.1 × 5.5 cm) 24-gauge predrilled brass sheet
+ 24-gauge brass sheet
+ One 35 mm plastic disc
+ One 36 mm brass filigree flower

Finished length

+ Varies

1. Make a 1.8 mm hole in the center of the plastic disc with the hole-punch pliers. Center the plastic disc on the front of the predrilled brass rectangle and place a mark through the hole onto the rectangle with a Sharpie. Punch a 1.8 mm hole at the mark. File the back of the hole with the salon board to remove any burrs.

2. Using a brass hammer and steel bench block, texture the outer edges of the brass sheet with a spiral metal stamp. Leave the areas that will be under the disc plain.

3. Rub African Bronze Gilders Paste on the front of the brass rectangle. Let dry, then reapply; once dry, buff with a soft cloth.

4. Using the disc cutter, cut a ¼" (6 mm) disc from the brass sheet. Using the spiral stamp, texture the disc as you did the rectangle. Make a hole in the center of the disc with the hole-punch pliers and file the back of the hole smooth. Apply African Bronze Gilders Paste, let dry, then buff.

5. Using metal shears, cut the filigree flower to 22 mm and file any rough edges. Punch a hole in the center of the filigree flower with the hole-punch pliers.

6. Scuff the front of the filigree flower with the salon board to prepare it for patina. Apply African Bronze Gilders Paste, let dry, and then buff.

7. Place the filigree flower, back side down, into a depression in the dapping block. Press down gently on the flower with your fingers to form it into a concave shape.

8. Thread a micro screw through the front of the textured disc, filigree flower, plastic disc, and brass rectangle. Thread a nut onto the back of the screw. Using the micro screwdriver and flat- or chain-nose pliers, tighten the screw and nut. Cut the back of the screw flush with the nut and file the rough edges. Place a drop of superglue on the back of the screw and nut.

9. Cut enough fabric cording to go around your head, plus 2" (5 cm). Thread the cording through the holes in the rectangle from front to back. Fold 1" (2.5 cm) of cording back onto itself and attach to the longer piece by coiling over both thicknesses with 18-gauge brass wire. Compress the coils with chain-nose pliers to secure. Trim any extra cording and add a drop of superglue to the cut ends.

Resources

Plastic disc: gulnurozdaglar.etsy.com. Brass sheet, 36 mm brass filigree flower: windspirit.etsy.com. Predrilled brass rectangle, micro screw/nut, 1.8 mm metal hole-punch pliers: objectsandelements.com. Gilders Paste: kabeladesign.com. Eyeglasses mini screwdriver: drugstore. Pepetools disc cutter, spiral stamp, scissor shears: beaducation.com.

Terra-cotta Sunset

Denise Peck

Tools

+ Disc cutter
+ Dapping block and punches
+ Ball-peen hammer
+ Butane micro torch
+ Annealing pan with pumice stone
+ Fireproof work surface (cookie sheet)
+ Quenching bowl
+ Utility pliers
+ 3 mm dimple-forming pliers
+ 1.8 mm metal hole-punch pliers
+ Flush cutters
+ Steel bench block
+ Round-nose pliers
+ Medium-grit sanding sponge
+ Sharpie marker or mandrel

Finished length

+ 1¾" (4.5 cm) including ear wire

Materials

+ Two 24-gauge 1¼" (3.2 cm) diameter copper discs or 24-gauge copper sheet
+ 4" (10 cm) of 20-gauge copper wire

1. If you're not using precut discs, cut two 1¼" (3.8 cm) discs from the copper sheet using the disc cutter. Place each disc back into the disc cutter at the ½" (1.3 cm) hole and cut a second hole close to the edge of each disc.

2. Place each disc into the appropriate-size depression in the dapping block and gently dome each disc with the matching punch.

3. Flame patina (see page 50) the discs with the butane micro torch to color the copper. Quench and dry.

4. Use the dimple-forming pliers to punch dimples around the edge of the hole in each disc.

5. Make a hole in the top of each disc for the ear wires using the hole-punch pliers.

6. Cut the 20-gauge wire in half and hammer ⅝" (1.5 cm) on one end of each wire into a paddle.

7. Use round-nose pliers to bend the flattened paddles up into a small hook. Thread a domed disc onto the hook and bend the length of the wire around a Sharpie or mandrel to form the ear wire; repeat for the other earring.

8. File the ends of the ear wires smooth and hammer the curves to work-harden them.

Resources

Swanstrom disc cutter, annealing pan with pumice stone: riogrande.com. Dimple-forming pliers: beadsmith.com. Copper discs: monsterslayer.com; beaducation.com.

Urban Cowgirl

Jane Dickerson

Materials

+ ¾" (2 cm) wide stampable black leather cuff
+ 26-gauge textured and patinated copper sheet
+ 5 faux turquoise 5mm snap rivets

Tools

+ Scissors
+ Center punch
+ Sheet of paper
+ Disc cutter
+ 100/180 coarse salon board
+ Ruler
+ Fine-point Sharpie marker
+ Power Punch pliers
+ Snap rivet setter
+ Steel bench block
+ Plastic mallet
+ 5 Pro-Polish pads

Finished size

+ Small 7" (18 cm), Medium–Large 7¾" (19.5 cm)

3. Mark the center of each disc with a Sharpie and make a hole at each mark using the Power Punch pliers and the $5/32$" (4 mm) punch. Center one $3/4$" (2 cm) disc over the dent you made in Step 1. Measure 1" (2.5 cm) from the center of the hole to the center of the next disc hole, placing $3/4$" (2 cm) discs on either side of the center disc and $5/8$" (1.5 cm) discs on the each end.

4. Once all the discs are in place, use a center punch to place a dent in the leather through the center of each disc hole. Remove the discs and make a hole at each mark with the Power Punch pliers and the $5/32$" (4 mm) punch.

5. Insert a turquoise snap rivet through the front of a $3/4$" (2 cm) disc and the front center hole in the leather cuff. Squeeze the back of the snap rivet in place until you feel it snap. Repeat to attach the other discs to the cuff.

6. Stack 5 Pro-Polish pads on a steel bench block. Turn the bracelet face down and center 1 snap rivet on the Pro-Polish pads. Using the snap rivet tool and a plastic/nylon hammer (make sure it is not a metal hammer) gently tap the back of the rivet until it compresses and is secure (see page 46). Rotate the riveting tool as you tap with the hammer to secure the rivets evenly. Repeat for all of the other snap rivets.

Resources

Pepetools disc cutter, leather cuff, snap rivets, snap rivet setter: beaducation.com. Textured sheet: melissamanley.etsy.com. 100/180 coarse salon board: bedbathandbeyond.com.

1. Test fit the leather cuff and cut off the extra snap with scissors, if needed. Fold the cuff in half, end to end, and find the center. Make a slight dent in the leather at that point with the center punch and try the bracelet on to check the location. Make a hole with the Power Punch pliers at the mark using the $5/32$" (4 mm) punch.

2. Place a sheet of paper over the front of the patinated copper sheet and place it, paper side down, in the disc cutter; this will protect the front of the sheet from any oil on the disc cutter. Cut three $3/4$" (2 cm) discs and two $5/8$" (1.5 cm) discs. File any rough edges with the salon board.

Ticket to Ride

Kristi Evenson

Materials

+ 22-gauge copper sheet
+ 16" (40.5 cm) of 20-gauge copper wire
+ 10mm closed copper ring
+ 40" (1.01 m) of 2 mm red leather cord
+ 2 antique-finish copper 10mm jump rings
+ 1 antique-finish copper 18.6mm lobster clasp

Tools

+ Digital image or photo
+ Kodak matte photo paper
+ Copier
+ Ruler
+ Fine-point Sharpie marker
+ Metal shears
+ Metal file
+ 1.5 mm metal hole-punch pliers
+ Texture hammer (optional)
+ Ball-peen hammer
+ Steel bench block
+ 220-grit sandpaper
+ Liver of sulfur
+ 0000 steel wool
+ Scissors
+ Butane lighter
+ Aluminum foil
+ Matte Mod Podge
+ 1" (2.5 cm) foam sponge brush
+ Krylon Matte Finish 1311 spray

+ 2 pairs of chain-nose pliers
+ Round-nose pliers
+ Wire cutters

Finished size

+ Pendant: 2¼" × 1" (5.5 × 2.5 cm)
+ Necklace: 19" (48.5 cm)

1. Decide what photo or image you wish to use. It works best if you keep the size of the image under 2" × 2" (5 × 5 cm) or it may wrinkle. Transfer the image onto a sheet of matte photo paper using a copier.

2. Measure the image and trace the exact size onto the 22-gauge sheet with the Sharpie marker. Cut out the shape with metal shears, leaving an additional ⅛–¼" (3–6 mm) border of copper showing. Slightly file the corners to remove the sharp points and file the edges smooth.

3. Make a hole in the top center of the piece with the hole-punch pliers.

4. Texture the front of the piece with a texture hammer or the ball end of the ball-peen hammer. Turn the piece over and lightly hammer the piece flat.

5. Use 220-grit sandpaper, moving in one direction, to clean and sand the front and back of the piece. Sand the edges as well for a nice clean edge.

6. Oxidize the copper piece, wire, and 10mm ring in liver of sulfur. Rinse and dry. Remove the excess patina with fine steel wool.

7. Using scissors, cut out the image on the matte photo paper. With the lighter, carefully burn small portions at a time around the edges of the image, until all the edges are burned. Lightly scrape the burned edges to remove any loose ash.

8. Place a sheet of aluminum foil on your work surface. Using a foam brush, apply a thin layer of Mod Podge onto the face of the copper piece and onto the back of the paper image. (This must be the matte version or results will differ.)

9. Carefully place the image in the center of the copper piece, as it will be difficult to move once contact is made. Don't be concerned if the hole at the top is covered. Dip the tip of your finger into the Mod Podge and starting in the center, smooth out the image to remove any bubbles or creases. Run the foam brush once again over the face of the piece to smooth out the finish.

10. Check the back of the piece and remove any Mod Podge that has accumulated. Set the piece aside on the aluminum foil to dry. Rinse out and dry the sponge brush for the next coat. Let each coat dry for about 30 minutes, then apply another coat of Mod Podge, for a total of three coats.

11. Once the piece is completely dry, lightly spray with the matte finish spray. (Again, it must be a matte finish.) Apply two coats, letting each dry between spraying. When the piece is completely dry, gently run the steel wool from top to bottom to smooth out the finish on the piece. If the hole at the top was covered while applying the image, carefully repunch it now from the back of the piece.

12. Cut 8" (20.5 cm) of copper wire. Make a 90° bend 1½" (3.8 cm) from one end of the wire with chain-nose pliers, then using round-nose pliers begin a wrapped loop. Slip the loop into the hole at the top of the pendant and wrap the loop closed.

13. Make another 90° bend about ¼" (6 mm) from the first loop, and make another wrapped loop, wrapping the remaining length of the wire around the ¼" (6 mm) space between the 2 loops. Hide the end of the wire into the wraps by pressing it in gently with chain-nose pliers.

14. Fold the cording in half. Insert the folded end into a copper jump ring and then insert the cut ends through the loop in the folded end, making a lark's head knot. Cut 4" (10 cm) of copper wire and make a coil around the leather, under the lark's head knot.

15. String the pendant onto the cut ends of the leather. Insert both cut ends through a jump ring and fold the leather ends over. Use the remaining 4" (10 cm) piece of wire to create a coil around the leather ends. Trim any leather ends that are showing, trim any excess wire, and press in the wire ends with chain-nose pliers.

Resources

Matte Mod Podge, spray matte finish: michaels.com.

Three's a Crowd

Denise Peck

Materials

+ 4 copper ⅝" (1.5 cm) cutwork discs with 2 holes
+ 2 copper ½" (1.3 cm) discs
+ 4 copper 6mm jump rings
+ 2 copper ear wires
+ 16 size 15° seed beads

Tools

+ Butane micro torch
+ Annealing pan with pumice stone
+ Fireproof work surface (cookie sheet)
+ Utility pliers
+ Quenching bowl
+ Dapping block and punches
+ 1.5 mm metal hole-punch pliers
+ Beading thread and needle
+ Scissors
+ 2 pairs of chain-nose pliers

Finished length

+ 2½" (6.5 cm) including the ear wire

1. Using the torch, flame patina (see page 50) all the copper discs.

2. Gently dome each disc in the dapping block with the matching punch (see page 35).

3. Make a hole on opposite sides of each ½" (1.3 cm) disc about 1 mm from the edge using the hole-punch pliers.

4. Use the jump rings to connect 2 cutwork discs together with a ½" (1.3 cm) disc in between.

5. Using the needle and thread, attach the seed beads to the top cutwork disc. Leaving a 2" (5 cm) tail, come up from the back of the disc with the needle, through one slit and down and out the next slit. Tie a knot in the back of the disc with the tail. Come back up through the first slit, add a seed bead, and go down and out the next slit. Come up through the third slit, add a seed bead, and go back down and out the second slit. Continue adding beads all the way around and tie off the thread in the back of the disc. Repeat for the second earring.

6. Add an ear wire to the top hole in each beaded cutwork disc.

Resources

Cutwork discs: echoartworks.com.

SilverWear

Jane Dickerson

Materials

+ 6" (15 cm) of sterling silver 5.04 × 1.71 mm dead-soft patterned wire
+ 9 sterling silver 16-gauge 6mm jump rings
+ 18.7mm sterling silver lobster clasp

Tools

+ Solderite pad
+ Cookie sheet
+ Butane micro torch
+ Utility pliers
+ Quenching bowl
+ Ruler
+ Heavy-duty flush cutters
+ 100/180 coarse salon board
+ Pro-Polish pad
+ Power Punch pliers
+ Stepped forming pliers (5, 7, and 10 mm)
+ Liver of sulfur
+ 2 pairs of flat-nose pliers
+ Rotary tumbler
+ Mixed stainless steel shot
+ Dawn dishwashing liquid

Finished size

+ 7" (18 cm)

1. Place the patterned wire on the Solderite pad, on top of the cookie sheet. Use the torch to anneal the wire (see page 24). Quench and dry.

2. With heavy-duty flush cutters, cut four 1¼" (3.2 cm) pieces of patterned wire. File and round all the ends with a 100/180 salon board.

3. Using the Power Punch pliers, punch a ³⁄₃₂" (2.4 mm) hole in the end of each piece of patterned wire. (Tip: Place a few Pro-Polish pads between the punch and the patterned wire to prevent it from being marred.) File the back of each piece with the salon board to remove the rough edges of the holes. Clean and polish the front of the links with a Pro-Polish pad to remove most of the fire scale. If you want to remove all of the fire scale, use pickle (see page 23).

4. Shape each link into a slight arch using the 10 mm jaw of stepped forming pliers as a mandrel.

5. Oxidize the lobster clasp and 9 sterling silver jump rings in a liver of sulfur solution (see page 49). Rinse and dry. Remove the excess patina with a Pro-Polish pad.

6. Using 2 pairs of flat-nose pliers, attach a jump ring between each link. Attach the lobster clasp to an end link with a jump ring. Make a chain with the remaining jump rings and attach the end jump ring to the other end of the bracelet.

7. Add a drop of Dawn to the water and mixed stainless steel shot in the tumbler. Tumble for 1 hour.

Resources

Patterned wire, jump rings, clasp, mixed stainless steel shot, Blazer micro torch, Solderite pad, liver of sulfur, Pro-Polish pads: riogrande.com. Tumbler: harborfreight.com. Stepped forming pliers, Power Punch pliers, heavy-duty flush cutters: beaducation.com.

Drink It All In

Cassie Donlen

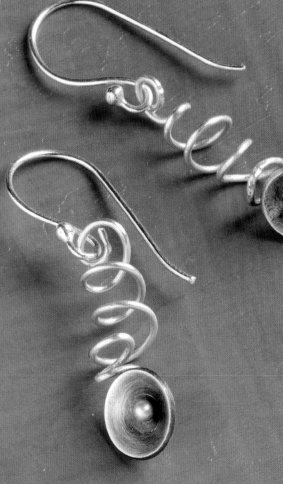

Tools

+ Fine-point Sharpie marker
+ 2-hole screw-down hole punch
+ Dapping block and punch
+ Brass mallet
+ Flush cutters
+ Butane micro torch
+ Charcoal block
+ Fireproof work surface (cookie sheet)
+ Heat-resistant tweezers
+ 6 mm mandrel
+ Round-nose pliers
+ Chain-nose pliers
+ Liver of sulfur
+ 0000 steel wool

Materials

+ 7" (18 cm) of 20-gauge fine silver round wire
+ 2 sterling silver 9.5mm 22-gauge discs
+ 2 size 11° silver-color seed beads
+ 2 sterling ear wires

Finished length

+ 1½" (3.8 cm) including the ear wire

3. Cut two 3½" (9 cm) pieces of 20-gauge fine silver wire. Use the micro torch to make 2 ball-end head pins (see page 25). Let cool.

4. Thread a head pin through the concave side of a disc. String a size 11° bead onto the head pin and press it against the back of the disc.

5. Use your fingers to hold the disc and seed bead in place. Bend the wire up 90° behind the bead so that it sits tightly against the bead and prevents it from sliding on the wire. Wrap the wire around the mandrel to make about 3 or 4 coils. Slightly spread the coils with your fingers until the desired look is achieved. Adjust the silver disc so that it is facing out instead of down. If the silver disc is very wobbly, slightly tighten the coil directly above the disc to make it smaller.

6. Use round-nose pliers to make a small loop on the end of each wire. Adjust the loop with chain-nose pliers so that it lies flat, which will make the silver discs face forward.

7. Oxidize the earrings in liver of sulfur; rinse and dry. Remove the excess patina with fine steel wool.

8. Attach an ear wire to the loop at the top of each coil.

Resources

Silver: riogrande.com.

1. Use a Sharpie marker to place a dot in the center of each of the silver discs. Make a hole at each dot using a 2-hole screw-down hole punch with the small ¹⁄₁₆" (2 mm) punch.

2. Place the silver disc into a dapping block in the depression that is closest to the same size as the disc. Use a ¹³⁄₃₂" (2.4 mm) punch and hammer it until it has a nice curve.

Drink It All In

Saucy
Denise Peck

Materials

- + 1 sterling 1" (2.5 cm) disc or 24-gauge sterling silver sheet
- + 7mm faceted cubed bead
- + 1 gunmetal 26-gauge 3" (7.5 cm) ball-end head pin
- + 5" (12.5 cm) of 1.5 mm green leather cord
- + 24" (61 cm) of silver chain and clasp

Tools

- + Disc cutter
- + Painter's tape
- + Brass patterned sheet
- + Utility ball-peen hammer
- + Steel bench block
- + Dapping block and punches
- + Pro-Polish pad
- + Brass mallet
- + Power Punch pliers
- + Chain-nose pliers
- + Round-nose pliers
- + Liver of sulfur
- + 0000 steel wool

Finished length

- + 24" (61 cm)

1. If you're not using a precut blank, cut a 1" (2.5 cm) disc from the sterling sheet with the disc cutter.

2. Tape the disc to the front of the patterned brass sheet. Place the disc, tape side up, on the steel bench block. Using the flat side of the utility ball-peen hammer, strike the silver disc firmly, covering the whole area of the disc to transfer the pattern from the sheet. Finish by hammering with the ball end of the hammer.

3. Remove the tape. Place the disc into the dapping block, texture side up. Cover the disc with a Pro-Polish pad to protect the texture and dap slightly with a brass mallet to dome the disc.

4. Oxidize the disc in liver of sulfur. Use fine steel wool to remove the excess oxidation.

5. Make a hole near the edge of the disc using the Power Punch pliers and the ⅛" (3.2 cm) punch.

6. String the bead onto the head pin and make a wrapped loop.

7. String the disc and the bead onto the leather cord and tie a knot to make a leather bail. Thread the chain through the bail.

Resources

Swanstrom disc cutter: riogrande.com. Green leather cord: antelopebeads.com. Brass patterned sheet: wiredarts.net. Chain: silkroadtreasures.com.

Calliope
Denise Peck

Tools

+ Fine-point Sharpie marker
+ Metal shears
+ Sanding block
+ Metal file
+ 1.5 mm metal hole-punch pliers
+ 1 mm hooked-jaw dimple pliers
+ Steel ring mandrel
+ Flush cutters
+ Round-nose pliers
+ Chain-nose pliers

Materials

+ Old piece of printed tin, flattened
+ 10–12 size 6° seed beads
+ 7" (18 cm) of 20-gauge sterling wire

Finished length

+ 1½" (3.8 cm)

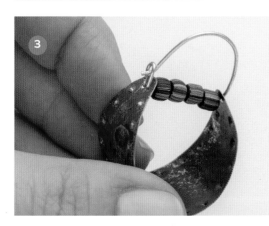

1. Trace the template onto the back of the tin and cut out the shape with metal shears. File all sharp edges with the sanding block and metal file if necessary. Repeat for the second earring.

2. Make a hole at both tips of both pieces of tin, 3–4mm from the end, with the hole-punch pliers. With dimple pliers, punch equally spaced dimples all along both edges of both pieces.

3. Gently fold the tin pieces around the large end of the ring mandrel, bringing the ends within ¾" (2 cm) of each other.

4. Cut the 20-gauge wire in half. Grasp one wire ¼" (6.5 mm) from one end with the tip of the round-nose pliers and make a hairpin bend. Make a 90° bend at the end of the hairpin bend with the long wire. Thread the wire through one earring, from the outside of the tin shape to the inside (Figure 1).

5. String enough seed beads onto the wire to fill the space between each side of the tin hoop (Figure 2). Exit the wire through the opposite hole.

6. Bend the wire straight up against the earring and gently fold the wire over your finger or a ring mandrel to shape the ear wire. Trim the wire short enough to pop into the hairpin bend and tip the end up so it will catch (Figure 3). File the end of the ear wire smooth. Repeat Steps 4–6 for the second earring.

Resources

1 mm hooked-jaw dimple pliers: beaducation.com.

Doorknocker

Keirsten Giles

Materials

+ 24- or 26-gauge copper sheet
+ 6" (15 cm) of 12-gauge copper wire
+ 12" (30.5 cm) of 20-gauge copper wire
+ 18" (45.5 cm) of 24-gauge copper wire
+ 2 copper $^5/_{32}$" × $^3/_{32}$" (4 × 2.4 mm) eyelets
+ 2 amber 7×12mm oval beads
+ 2 dark topaz 4mm faceted round Czech fire-polished beads

Tools

+ Metal shears
+ Metal file
+ Butane micro torch
+ Annealing pan with pumice stone
+ Fireproof work surface (cookie sheet)
+ Utility pliers
+ Quenching bowl
+ Pickle
+ Mini crock
+ Copper tongs
+ 0000 steel wool
+ Brass texture sheet or coin
+ Painter's tape
+ Heavy utility hammer
+ Steel bench block
+ Ultrafine sandpaper
+ Large bail-forming pliers (9 mm)
+ Chain-nose pliers
+ Flat-nose pliers
+ Chasing hammer

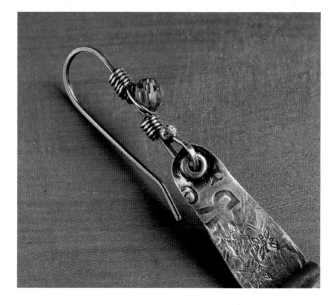

+ Ruler
+ Fine-point Sharpie marker
+ Stepped forming pliers (1.75–8 mm)
+ Round-nose pliers
+ Bent-nose pliers
+ 2-hole screw-down punch
+ Round needle file
+ Center punch or flare tool
+ Flush cutters
+ Liver of sulfur
+ Rotary tumbler
+ Mixed stainless steel shot

Finished length

+ 2$^{15}/_{16}$" (7.5 cm)

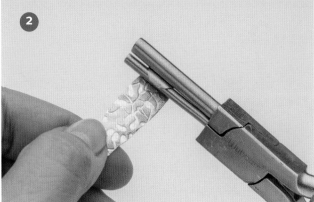

1. Using the Doorknocker template on page 140, cut two pieces from the copper sheet with metal shears and file the edges smooth. Anneal, quench, and pickle the pieces. Dry, then clean them with steel wool.

2. Texture the pieces with brass texture sheets or coins (see page 29). Anneal again, quench, pickle, dry, and clean with steel wool. Clean up any irregularities in the edges caused by the texturing process with a metal file and ultrafine sandpaper.

3. Using the 9 mm barrel of the large bail-forming pliers, create 2 rings from the 12-gauge copper wire. Flatten the rings slightly on the bench block with the chasing hammer, then form them into elongated ovals. Grasp each ring with chain-nose pliers at the 9 o'clock position (or 3 o'clock position if you are left-handed), with the seam at the 6 o'clock position, and lightly tap with the chasing hammer, on a bench block, until the shape starts to flatten into an oval (Figure 1). To keep the oval from being lopsided, turn the ring around, grasp it again at 9 o'clock, and hammer a little more in the same way. Keep flattening until the inner diameter is about 12 mm, just big enough to slide over the wider end of the piece. If the cut ends of the jump ring have opened or curled, squeeze them at the seam with chain-nose pliers

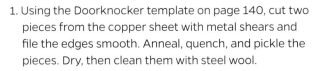

to straighten them out again. It will eventually be slightly straighter across the top and rounder across the bottom.

4. When the ovals are the right shape and size, check the seams. If the seams are open, stand the ring on its side on the bench block and tap each end lightly with the hammer until the join comes together again.

5. Draw a line with the Sharpie across the textured side of the bottom of each metal piece, 10 mm from the bottom edge. With the textured side of the piece facing you, using the 2 mm barrel of the stepped forming pliers, curl each piece up toward you at the line to form a U shape (Figure 2). Make sure the two pieces are still even with each other.

6. Slide an oval ring into the curl, with the seam of the ring hidden inside. With round- or bent-nose pliers, continue to curl the metal in toward the body of the piece. Curl both sides evenly with pliers. Tighten each curl with flat-nose pliers. When the curls are completely tightened, the oval rings will not move (Figure 3). Make sure the earrings are still even with each other.

7. Using the Sharpie, make a mark at the top of each piece for the eyelets, centering the marks 3 mm

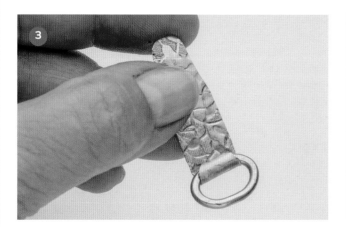

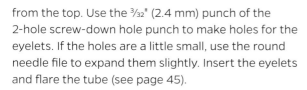

from the top. Use the ³⁄₃₂" (2.4 mm) punch of the 2-hole screw-down hole punch to make holes for the eyelets. If the holes are a little small, use the round needle file to expand them slightly. Insert the eyelets and flare the tube (see page 45).

8. Using the 20-gauge wire, make four 3" (7.5 cm) ball-end head pins (see page 25). Thread an oval bead onto a head pin and attach it to the bottom of one earring with a wrapped loop; repeat for the other earring.

9. With the chasing hammer, slightly flatten about 1" (2.5 cm) of the shaft of each remaining head pin starting from the ball end. The flattened shape of the shaft will hold the wire wrap in place better than a round shape. Using the 2 mm barrel of the stepped forming pliers, grasp the head pin just under the ball and bend it into a U shape; repeat for the other ear wire. Make sure both U shapes are even with each other. Attach the ear wires to the top of the earrings.

10. Using 9" (23 cm) of 24-gauge copper wire and leaving a 2" (5 cm) tail at the bottom, wrap the wire four times around the base of the head pin, just above where the ball is.

11. Thread a 4mm bead onto the longer wire as close to the head pin as you can. Holding the bead in place against the head pin, wrap the wire twice around the head pin, above the bead. Wrap the wire in a circle around the bead twice. Then, wrap the head pin five more times above the bead, wrapping over the existing wraps. Trim the wire on the back and pinch in the end with chain-nose pliers.

12. Wrap the 2" (5 cm) tail at the bottom of the bead over the first wraps a few times, completing a double wrap on the bottom of the bead as well. Trim the excess wire and pinch in the end.

13. With one earring facing you, grasp the head pin just above the wrapped bead with the 7 mm barrel of the stepped forming pliers. Make sure the beaded portion of the head pin is flush against the barrel of the pliers, then bend the head pin over the pliers to create the ear wire. Make sure the ear wires are identical, adjusting as necessary, and making sure each earring hangs at the same length.

14. Oxidize the earrings with liver of sulfur and tumble to polish.

Resources

Copper sheet and wire: monsterslayer.com. Eyelets: riogrande.com. Coins: joelscoins.com. Amber beads: firemountaingems.com. Czech beads: fusionbeads.com.

Band It!

Cassie Donlen

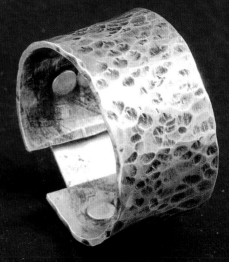

Materials

+ 10 x 1mm flat sterling wire*
+ 21 mm long strip of ¼" (6 mm) 28-gauge fine silver bezel wire
+ 4 aluminum ¹⁄₁₆" × ³⁄₃₂" (2 x 2.4mm Crafted Findings rivets

See Step 1 to determine the length of flat wire needed for your ring size.

Tools

+ Ruler
+ Metal shears
+ Metal file
+ Sandpaper (various grits)
+ Ball-peen hammer
+ Steel bench block
+ Butane micro torch
+ Charcoal block
+ Fireproof work surface (cookie sheet)
+ Utility pliers
+ Quenching bowl
+ Large stepped forming pliers (16 mm)
+ Steel ring mandrel
+ Rawhide mallet
+ Fine-point Sharpie marker
+ 2-hole screw-down hole punch
+ Riveting hammer
+ Liver of sulfur
+ 0000 steel wool

Finished size

+ Varies

1. Use metal shears to cut a strip of flat sterling wire the length of your desired ring size. For a size 5, cut it about 49 mm long; size 6 is 51.5 mm long; size 7 is 54 mm long; size 8 is 56.5 mm long; size 9 is 60 mm long; size 10 is 61.5 mm long. The final ring size will be confirmed as the design progresses. File the edges smooth.

2. Using the ball end of a ball-peen hammer, gently hammer one side of the wire to texture it. This will stretch out the wire and lengthen it slightly. Anneal the wire (see page 24).

3. Wrap the wire on the middle step (16 mm) of a pair of large stepped forming pliers until it forms a circle. There should be a 3–6 mm gap between the two ends. Slide the ring onto a steel ring mandrel and use a rawhide mallet to tap the edges into the final round shape if needed.

4. Determine the current ring size while it is sitting on the mandrel. If the size needs to be adjusted, squeeze or stretch the gap in the wire to manipulate it to the desired size. There should be a 3–6 mm gap between the two wire ends. If the ring is too large, use metal shears to trim the wire and reshape it. If it is too small, pound the wire with a rawhide mallet while it is still on the ring mandrel or make the gap in the ring slightly larger by pushing the ring down onto a larger ring size on the mandrel.

5. Use metal shears to cut a 21 mm piece of bezel wire. File the edges smooth. Use a Sharpie to make two vertical dots, evenly spaced, about 3 mm from the outer edge on each end of the wire. Make a hole at each of the dots with the smaller $\frac{1}{16}$" (2 mm) size of a 2-hole screw-down hole-punch. File the back of the holes smooth.

6. Take the small strip of bezel wire and form it over the ring where the gap is located. Center the wire so that there are equal amounts of bezel wire on each side of the gap. Gently curve the wire with your fingers so that it follows the curvature of the ring. Hold the bezel wire in place with your fingers. Using the small end of the 2-hole screw-down hole punch, screw the punch down into one of the previous punched holes of the bezel wire, and then continue to punch a hole into the ring to make a hole for a rivet. File the holes smooth.

7. Insert a Crafted Findings rivet with the head side going through from the inside of the ring. With the rivet in place, slide the ring onto the ring mandrel so that the end of the rivet protrudes on the outside of the ring. Use a riveting hammer to flare the tube on the outside section of the ring. Repeat Steps 6 and 7 for the second hole on the same side of the bezel wire.

8. Before riveting the holes on the opposite side of the bezel wire, confirm that the ring is the appropriate size. If it is too large, use your fingers to gently squeeze together the gap in the ring and hold in place when making the rivet holes on the opposite side of the ring. If the ring is too small, gently stretch the gap area apart to enlarge the ring. Repeat Steps 6 and 7 to form the final rivets on the other side.

9. Oxidize the ring in liver of sulfur. Buff the ring with fine steel wool to give it an antique silver finish.

Resources

Flat sterling wire: hauserandmiller.com. Bezel wire: riogrande.com. Large stepped pliers: beaducation.com. Rivets: craftedfindings.com.

Cummerbund
Kerry Bogert

Materials

+ 5" (12.5 cm) of ½" (1.3 cm) wide 24-gauge flat sterling strip or 24-gauge sheet metal
+ 14" (35.5 cm) of sterling 16-gauge round dead soft wire
+ 6' (1.8 m) of colored copper 20-gauge round wire

Tools

+ Metal shears
+ Ruler
+ Metal file
+ Bracelet mandrel
+ Nylon mallet
+ 4 mm bail-forming pliers
+ Sanding sponges, various grits
+ Coiling Gizmo
+ Flush cutters
+ Chain-nose pliers
+ Round-nose pliers
+ Chasing hammer
+ Steel bench block
+ Rotary tumbler
+ Mixed stainless steel shot

Finished size

+ 8" (20.5 cm)

totally personal preference whether your loop rolls toward the inside of the band or toward the outside. I happen to like the shadow line that rolling toward the outside makes.

4. For an etched look, use three coarse grades of sanding pads and randomly rub in different directions all over the surface.

5. Using the Coiling Gizmo, make 2 coils from the 20-gauge colored copper wire, each 3" (7.5 cm) long. Slide one of the coils onto a 7" (18 cm) piece of 16-gauge round silver wire. Center the coil on the wire and then pass it through the loop in the flat wire. Center the coil in the loop so that there are equal amounts of coil showing on either side (Figure 2).

6. Bring the ends of the coiled area together. Wrap one end of the 16-gauge wire around the other just beyond the coil, as if making a wrapped loop. Trim the excess wire and file smooth. Trim the remaining wire to about ⅝" (1.5 cm) and use round-nose pliers to form a simple loop. Form a slight arch in the coiled area to follow the curve of a wrist.

7. Repeat the previous steps with the second coil on the opposite side of the bracelet, stopping at the point where you need to form a simple loop. Instead, use the round-nose pliers to shape the tail wire into a hook for a clasp. Trim any excess wire beyond the clasp and file the cut end smooth (Figure 3).

8. With a chasing hammer and bench block, flatten the arch of the hook. *Note:* So that the clasp hugs your wrist, doesn't easily come loose, and doesn't snag on things, be sure to position the hook so it is lying flat against your wrist. The catch side of the clasp—the loop—should be perpendicular to that. The loop is small enough that it shouldn't stick out too far from your wrist.

9. Tumble for 45 to 60 minutes to further work-harden the metal band and polish all the wire.

Resources

Sterling strip or sheet metal: riogrande.com. Colored wire: parawire.com.

1. Cut a 5" (12.5 cm) length of ½" (1.3 cm) wide flat sterling strip (or cut a 5" × ½" [12.5 × 1.3 cm] strip from a piece of sheet metal). File the corners round and smooth the edges.

2. Wrap the ½" (1.3 cm) strip around the bracelet mandrel and work-harden with the nylon mallet, except for ¾" (2 cm) on each end. Spend several minutes hammering the wire to make it very stiff and hold its shape. Focus the strikes on the back area of the band.

3. Grasp one end of the flat wire in the jaws of the bail-forming pliers. Start to roll the wire around the pliers (Figure 1). Roll about halfway and then flip the wire around and roll again. Repeat on the other end. It is

Corbel

Keirsten Giles

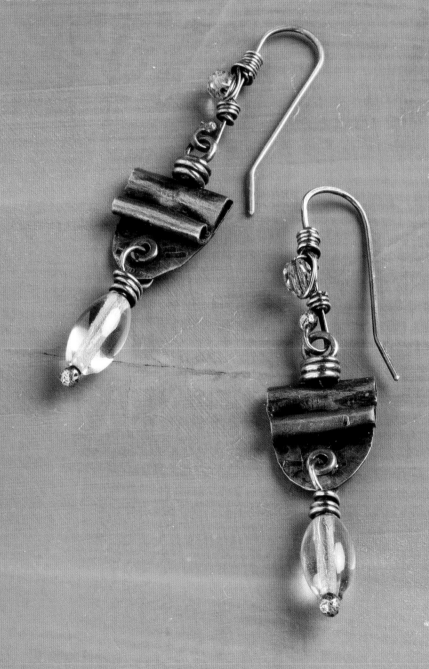

Materials

+ 26-gauge copper sheet
+ 6" (15 cm) of 18-gauge copper wire
+ 12" (30.5 cm) of 20-gauge copper wire
+ 18" (45.5 cm) of 24-gauge copper wire
+ 2 copper ⁵⁄₃₂" × ³⁄₃₂" (4 × 2.4 mm) eyelets
+ 2 alexandrite 4mm round faceted Czech fire-polished beads
+ 2 alexandrite 12×7mm oval Czech pressed-glass beads

Tools

+ Metal shears
+ Metal file
+ Butane micro torch
+ Annealing pan with pumice stone
+ Fireproof work surface (cookie sheet)
+ Utility pliers
+ Quenching bowl
+ Pickle
+ Mini crock
+ Copper tongs
+ 0000 steel wool
+ Brass texture sheet or coin
+ Painter's tape
+ Heavy utility hammer
+ Steel bench block
+ Ultrafine sandpaper
+ Stepped forming pliers (1.75–8 mm)
+ Fine-point Sharpie marker
+ Ruler
+ 1.5 mm metal hole-punch pliers
+ Flat-nose pliers
+ Round-nose pliers
+ Chain-nose pliers
+ 2-hole screw down punch
+ Round needle file
+ Center punch or flaring tool
+ Chasing hammer
+ Flush cutters
+ Cup bur (optional)
+ Liver of sulfur
+ Rotary tumbler
+ Mixed stainless steel shot

Finished length

+ 2½" (6.5 cm)

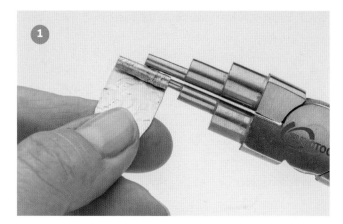

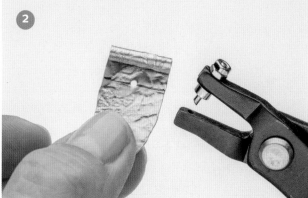

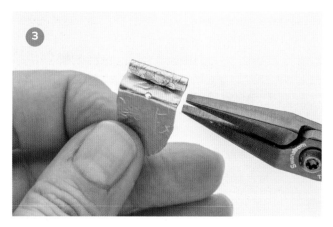

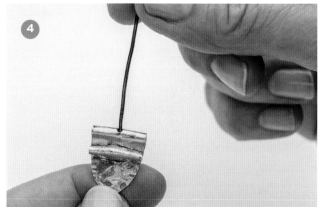

1. Using the Corbel template on page, cut two pieces from the copper sheet and file the edges smooth. Anneal, quench, pickle, and dry, then clean with steel wool.

2. Texture the pieces with brass texture sheets or coins (see page 29). Anneal again, quench, pickle, and dry, then clean with steel wool. Clean up any irregularities in the edges caused by the texturing process with a metal file and ultrafine sandpaper.

3. Using 18-gauge wire, create two 3" (7.5 cm) ball-end head pins with the torch. Pickle and clean with steel wool. Hammer each ball slightly flat. Set aside.

4. With the smooth side of the sheet facing you, grasp the straight edge of one copper piece with the

1.75 mm barrel of the stepped forming pliers. Create a tight curl, curling toward you. Repeat on the other piece, making sure both curls are uniform and both pieces are still the same length, about 23 mm long (Figure 1).

5. Using a Sharpie, draw a line straight across the smooth side of one piece, 4 mm from the bottom edge of the curl; repeat on the other piece. Make a hole exactly in the center of each line with the hole-punch pliers (Figure 2).

6. With the smooth side of one piece facing you and the curl at the top, grasp the piece with flat-nose pliers along the line, just at the bottom edge of the hole. Bend it away from you 90°, being sure to keep the hole centered at the top of the fold (Figure 3).

7. Insert a flattened ball-end head pin into the hole, with the ball inside the fold; fold the rest of the way over with your fingers and pliers. Repeat Steps 6 and 7 with the other piece, making sure both pieces remain equal lengths (Figure 4).

8. Create a wrapped loop with the protruding ends of each head pin, being sure to keep both loops the same size and length.

9. Using the Sharpie, make a mark on the front of each piece, centered near the bottom edge and about 3 mm from the bottom. Use the ³⁄₃₂" (2.4 mm) punch on the 2-hole screw-down punch to make a hole in each earring for the eyelets. If the holes are too small, use the round needle file to expand them slightly. Insert the eyelets and flare the back of the tube (see page 45).

10. Make four 3" (7.5 cm) copper ball-end head pins (see page 25) with 20-gauge wire. Thread an oval bead onto one head pin and attach it to the riveted hole at the bottom of one earring with a wrapped loop; repeat for the other earring. Make sure the earrings remain the same length.

11. With the chasing hammer, slightly flatten about 1" (2.5 cm) of the shaft of each remaining head pin starting from the ball end. The flattened shape of the shaft will hold the wire wrap in place better than a round shape. Using the 2 mm barrel of the stepped forming pliers, grasp one head pin just under the ball and bend

it into a U shape; repeat for the other head pin. Make sure both U shapes are even with each other. Thread the head pins onto the top of the earrings.

12. Using 9" (23 cm) of 24-gauge copper wire and leaving a 2" (5 cm) tail at the bottom, wrap the wire four times around the base of one head pin, just above where the ball is.

13. Thread a 4mm bead onto the longer wire, as close to the head pin as you can. Holding the bead in place against the head pin, wrap the wire twice around the head pin, above the bead. Wrap the wire in a circle around the bead twice. Then, wrap the head pin five more times, above the bead, wrapping over the existing wraps. Trim the wire on the back and pinch in the end with chain-nose pliers.

14. Wrap the 2" (5 cm) tail at the bottom of the bead over the first wraps a few times, completing a double wrap on the bottom of the bead as well. Trim the excess wire and pinch in the end.

15. With one earring facing you, grasp the head pin just above the wrapped bead with the 7 mm barrel of the stepped forming pliers. Make sure the beaded portion of the head pin is flush up against the barrel of the pliers, then bend the head pin over the pliers to create the ear wire. Make sure the ear wires are identical, adjusting as necessary, and making sure each earring hangs at the same length. Repeat Steps 12–15 to make the other ear wire (Figure 5).

16. Gently work-harden the ear wires with the chasing hammer on the bench block. Trim the ear wires as needed and finish the end with a cup bur or sandpaper.

17. As long as you have not used any beads that are vulnerable to liver of sulfur (or tumbling if you're going to tumble polish), you can oxidize the entire earring and polish.

Resources

Copper sheet and wire: monsterslayer.com.
Eyelets: riogrande.com. Coins: joelscoins.com.
Czech beads: fusionbeads.com.

Shattered

Denise Peck

Materials

+ ½" × ½" (1.3 × 1.3 cm) pottery shard
+ 24-gauge sterling sheet
+ 6–8" (15–20.5 cm) of 16-gauge silver-filled or sterling wire
+ 8" (20.5 cm) of 22-gauge sterling wire
+ 6 sterling 3mm faceted cube beads
+ 15" (38 cm) of sterling 4mm oval link chain
+ 2 sterling 6mm jump rings
+ Sterling lobster clasp

Tools

+ Fine-point Sharpie marker
+ Ruler
+ Metal shears
+ Metal file
+ Sanding sponge
+ Painter's tape
+ Brass texture sheet
+ Utility ball-peen hammer
+ Steel bench block
+ Butane micro torch
+ Annealing pan with pumice stone
+ Fireproof work surface (cookie sheet)
+ Utility pliers
+ Quenching bowl
+ Pickle
+ Mini crock
+ Copper tongs
+ 1.8 mm metal hole-punch pliers
+ Heavy-duty flush cutters
+ Steel anvil
+ Liver of sulfur
+ 0000 steel wool
+ Chain-nose pliers
+ Round-nose pliers
+ Rotary tumbler
+ Mixed stainless steel shot

Finished size

+ Necklace: 16" (40.5 cm)
+ Pendant: 1" × 1" (2.5 × 2.5 cm)

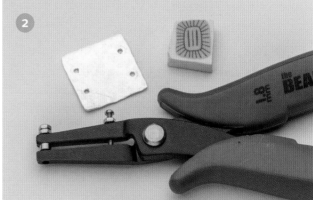

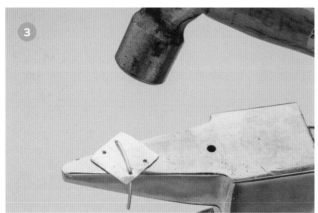

1. Place the pottery shard on the sterling sheet and draw a shape around it with the Sharpie, leaving at least a ¼" (6.5 mm) border. You can make it any shape you want (Figure 1).

2. Cut the sterling sheet along the lines with metal shears, forming the back plate. File the edges smooth.

3. Tape the back plate to the front of the brass texture sheet. On the bench block, hammer the sterling piece firmly with the utility ball-peen hammer to transfer the texture (see page 29).

4. Remove the tape. Anneal the back plate with the torch (see page 24), pickle, rinse, and dry.

5. Center the shard on the back plate and mark the edges at four places where you want the prongs to come up and over the shard. Make 4 holes with the 1.8 mm hole-punch pliers at the marks (Figure 2).

6. Cut the 16-gauge wire in half. Thread one piece of wire up through one hole from the back, leaving about ½" (1.3 cm) extending out the front. Bend the long end of the wire flush against the back of the back plate. Bend the end up through the hole diagonally across from the first hole. Turn the piece upside down on the anvil so the wire straddles the horn, then hammer the back wire flat (Figure 3).

7. Thread the second wire through the remaining holes as in Step 6. Place the back plate and wires over the end of the anvil again and hammer both the wires flat against the back of the back plate (Figure 4).

8. Oxidize the piece in liver of sulfur; rinse and dry. Remove the excess oxidation with steel wool.

9. Place the pottery shard on the back plate and begin to fold the prongs over it with chain-nose pliers, just to assess the lengths. You'll need about ⅛" (3 mm) more than the thickness of the shard for each prong. Trim the excess wire (Figure 5).

10. Remove the shard. Straighten the prongs and file the ends smooth. Place the prongs on the anvil and hammer ⅛" (3 mm) on the ends into a paddle. Replace the shard and fold the prongs snugly over the front. Gently hammer the prongs against the shard—gently (Figure 6)!

11. Make 2 holes at the top of the piece for the chain with the 1.5 mm hole-punch pliers. Tumble the piece for 30 minutes to 1 hour to polish.

12. Cut the 22-gauge wire in half. String 3 silver beads on one wire and begin a wire-wrapped loop on one end. Begin a larger wire-wrapped loop on the other end. Thread the larger loop through one hole on the top of the pendant and wrap closed. Repeat with the other piece of wire.

13. Cut the chain in half. Attach one end to one open loop from Step 12 and wrap it closed. Repeat with the other length of chain.

14. Attach a jump ring to one end of the necklace and use a second jump ring to connect the lobster clasp to the other end of the necklace.

Resources

Sterling wire and sheet: riogrande.com.
Sterling faceted cube beads: singarajaimports.com.
Pottery shard: ebay.com.

Sedona

Keirsten Giles

Materials

+ 24- or 26-gauge copper sheet
+ 4" (10 cm) of 16-gauge copper wire
+ 2" (5 cm) of 18-gauge copper wire
+ 13" (33 cm) of 22-gauge copper wire
+ 18" (45.5 cm) of 24-gauge copper wire
+ 30 × 40mm flat pear rainbow onyx pendant
+ 7½" (19 cm) of sari silk ribbon
+ 33" (84 cm) of antique copper 3.2mm ball chain
+ 2 antique copper 3.2 mm ball-tip connectors
+ 2 copper 14mm jump rings
+ 1 copper 8mm jump ring
+ 2 copper 5.5mm jump rings
+ 3 copper 6mm jump rings
+ ⁷⁄₁₆" (1.1 cm) #4 copper cut tack

Tools

+ Metal shears
+ Metal file
+ Annealing pan with pumice
+ Fireproof work surface (cookie sheet)
+ Utility pliers
+ Quenching bowl
+ Pickle
+ Mini crock
+ Copper tongs
+ 0000 steel wool
+ Brass texture sheet or coin
+ Painter's tape
+ Steel bench block
+ Heavy utility hammer
+ Stepped forming pliers (2 mm, 4 mm)
+ Chasing hammer
+ Disc cutter
+ 1.2 mm metal hole-punch pliers
+ Dapping block and punches
+ Liver of sulfur
+ Rotary tumbler
+ Mixed stainless steel shot
+ Fine-point Sharpie marker
+ Ruler
+ Medium bail-forming pliers (3 mm, 5 mm)
+ Fine- and ultrafine-grit sandpaper
+ Screw-down hole punch
+ Round needle file
+ Heavy-duty flush cutters
+ Bent-nose pliers
+ Chain-nose pliers
+ Nylon-jaw pliers

Finished length

+ 24¾" (63 cm)

1. Using the Sedona fold-over bail template on page 140, cut out the piece from the copper sheet using metal shears and file the edges. Anneal, quench, pickle, and dry the piece, then clean it with steel wool. Texture the piece with a brass texture sheet or coin.

2. Using stepped forming pliers, create a figure-eight shape with about 2" (5.1 cm) of 16-gauge wire; make one loop with the 2 mm barrel and the other loop with the 4 mm barrel. Flush cut the excess wire. Flatten the figure eight slightly with a chasing hammer. After hammering it will be about 14 mm long. Set aside (Figure 1).

3. Create 5 ball-end head pins (see page 25): four 2" (5 cm) long from 22-gauge wire and one 2" (5 cm) long from 18-gauge wire. Pickle, dry, and clean with steel wool. Set aside.

4. Cut a ½" (1.3 cm) circle from 24- or 26-gauge copper sheet with the disc cutter. Anneal, quench, pickle, and dry the disc, then clean it with steel wool. Texture the disc with a brass texture sheet or coin (see page 29).

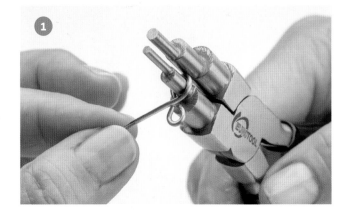

5. Make a hole in the center of the disc with the hole-punch pliers. With the textured side facing up, dome the disc with a dapping block and punch (see page 35). Oxidize and tumble. Set aside.

6. Using the Sharpie, draw a straight line across the center of the oval from Step 1, on the smooth side. Use the 3 mm barrel of the medium bail-forming pliers to fold the oval over on itself, with the textured side out (Figure 2). The folded edge will be the top of the bail. Even up the edges as needed with a file. Sand it smooth with fine- and then ultrafine-grit sandpaper.

7. Using the screw-down hole punch, make a ³⁄₃₂" (2.4 mm) hole centered along the edge of the bottom curved portion, about 5 mm from the edge, just large enough for a #4 copper cut tack, which you will use for a rivet. Use the round needle file to ream the hole until the tack just fits.

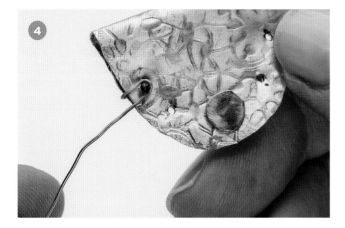

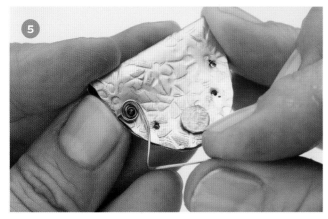

9. Use the hole-punch pliers to make 4 holes along the sides of the oval, 4 mm in from the edge, punching through both thicknesses of the metal. Space the first holes about 5 mm from the tack on either side, then the next 2 holes 7 mm from those.

10. To create a rosette, insert a 22-gauge ball-end head pin, with the ball on the same side as the tack head (these will form the front of your bail). Pull the ball tight against the metal and bend the wire tail tightly over the edge of the metal and around the ball, using bent-nose pliers to give it a tight, crisp bend around the edge of the metal. Wrap the tail of the head pin around the ball three times, creating a spiral (Figures 4 and 5).

11. Snip off the wire with flush cutters at the outer edge of the rosette and tuck in the end with bent-nose pliers. Repeat Steps 10 and 11 for the remaining 3 holes. Oxidize and tumble the finished bail.

12. To attach the focal stone to the bail, take the 2" (5 cm) 18-gauge head pin and slide on the textured disc from Step 5, with the head of the pin inside the cup shape of the disc. Insert the head pin into the hole of the stone and bend the tail of the head pin up sharply, flat against the back of the stone. Snip off the tail of the head pin leaving about 22 mm above the top of the stone. Use the ball end of the chasing hammer to flatten the end of the head pin into a slight paddle. Coil the head pin with 24-gauge copper wire, starting at the back as close to the stone as possible and coiling up to the paddle end (the paddle end will be hidden behind the copper disc). Snip off the excess 24-gauge wire and pinch in the end with chain-nose pliers. You can tumble polish the stone portion at this time if you wish, or you can attach it to the bail now and hand-polish it.

13. Using the 3 mm barrel of the medium bail-forming pliers, bend the coiled head pin partway up over the top of the stone, slide it onto the loop on the bail, and bend the rest of the head pin down, hiding it behind the cop-

8. Insert the smaller loop of the figure eight between the flaps of metal, centering it inside and between the drilled holes. Insert the tack through the hole, through the figure-eight loop, and out through the other hole. If the bail already has a "front," make sure the finished tack head is in front. Make sure the tack is inserted all the way, with the tack head flush against the metal. Use heavy-duty cutters to cut off the pointed end of the tack, leaving about 2 mm sticking up above the metal. Begin hammering the end of the tack flat with the chasing hammer, making sure to keep the figure eight straight as you hammer, and readjusting as needed until it is securely in place (Figure 3).

per disc. Hand-polish the wire wrapping and the ball of the pin if you elected not to tumble this portion separately. Oxidize with liver of sulfur and tumble to polish.

14. Flatten the 14mm jump rings slightly with the chasing hammer on the bench block. Pinch the jump rings closed if they opened up during hammering. Cut the 24-gauge wire in half and coil one piece a few times around the seam of each jump ring to hide it. Trim the wire and pinch in the ends with chain-nose pliers. Repeat this step with the 8mm jump ring.

15. To make the toggle bar (see top right), place the middle of the remaining 2" (5 cm) piece of 16-gauge wire over the 3 mm barrel of the stepped forming pliers and wrap each side of the wire around the jaw, forming a loop in the middle. Check the size of the toggle, passing it through a 14mm jump ring. If needed, trim the ends, leaving enough excess wire on each end to create a ball with the torch. Form a ball on each end of the toggle bar. Flatten each ball with a chasing hammer. Coil 24-gauge wire on each side of the toggle bar. Trim the wire and pinch in the ends with chain-nose pliers.

16. Cut two ⅛" × 3" (3 × 7.5 cm) strips of copper sheet. Round the ends with shears and file smooth. Texture with a brass texture sheet or coin. Anneal, quench, pickle, and dry, then clean with steel wool. Using the 5 mm barrel of the medium bail-forming pliers, shape each of the strips into a coil. Oxidize the coils, all the jump rings, and toggle bar. Hand-polish with steel wool.

17. Thread the sari silk ribbon through the bail, then thread one coil and a 14mm wire-wrapped jump ring onto each end of the ribbon. On one end, fold the ribbon over the jump ring and wrap it tightly with 2½" (6.5 cm) of 22-gauge wire. Slide the coil over the wire wrap to hide it and tighten the coil in place with nylon-jaw pliers. Repeat on the other side. Attach the ball-tip connectors to each end of the chain. Thread one end of the chain through one 14mm jump ring

and bring the ball-tip ends together. Attach a 5.5mm jump ring to each hole in the connectors and, before closing the jump rings, attach them to the 8mm wire-wrapped jump ring; close the jump rings. Connect three 6mm jump rings in a chain, attaching one end to the toggle bar and the other end to the 8mm wire-wrapped jump ring. Connect the toggle bar to the 14mm wire-wrapped jump ring on the other side of the necklace.

Resources

Copper sheet: monsterslayer.com. Coins: joelscoins.com. Tacks: acehardware.com. Sari silk ribbon: jmozart.etsy .com. Onyx pendant: gemmall.com. Ball chain, ball-tip connectors: chaingallery.com.

Impression

Kerry Bogert

Materials

+ 24-gauge copper sheet metal, or ½" wide (1.3 cm) 24-gauge flat copper strip

+ 4' (1.2 m) of sterling 24-gauge round dead-soft wire

+ 14" (35.5 cm) of sterling 18-gauge round half-hard wire

+ 1 pair of sterling French ear wires

Tools

+ Metal shears
+ Ruler
+ Nylon mallet
+ Steel bench block
+ Metal file
+ Sanding sponges, medium and fine grit
+ Metal alphabet stamps
+ Brass mallet or utility hammer
+ 1.25 mm metal hole-punch pliers
+ Round-nose pliers
+ Chain-nose pliers
+ Fine-point Sharpie marker
+ Washi tape or transparent tape roll or other ½" (1.3 cm) wide wedge
+ Flush cutter
+ Chasing hammer
+ Liver of sulfur
+ Pro-Polish pad

Finished length

+ 2¾" (7 cm) including the ear wire

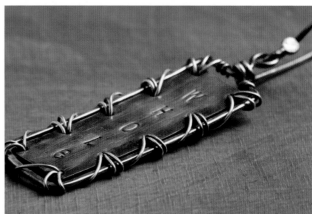

1. Using metal shears, cut a 3" × ½" (7.5 × 1.3 cm) strip of copper sheet. If the metal curls as you cut it, use the nylon mallet to gently hammer it flat. Measure and cut the strip into two 1½" (3.8 cm) pieces, or plates.

2. With the metal file and sanding sponge, remove any sharp edges on the copper plates. Texture or stamp a word onto each plate with the alphabet stamps and brass mallet or utility hammer (see page 28).

3. Use a ruler and Sharpie to mark the spacing, then make 5 evenly spaced holes down each side of both plates with the hole-punch pliers (Figure 1).

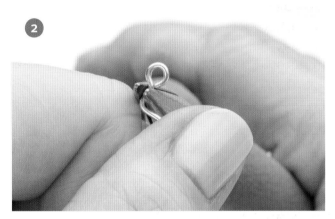

4. Using round-nose pliers, form a small simple loop at the end of a 7" (18 cm) piece of 18-gauge wire. Use the tip of the chain-nose pliers to create a ⅛" (3 mm) space below the simple loop, then make a 90° bend in the wire (Figure 2).

5. Line up the loop just formed with the top center of the metal plate. With the Sharpie, mark the wire at the corner of the plate. Pivot the wire to mark it at the second corner, then the third, and then the fourth. Use chain-nose pliers to form 90° bends in the wire at each spot marked (Figure 3).

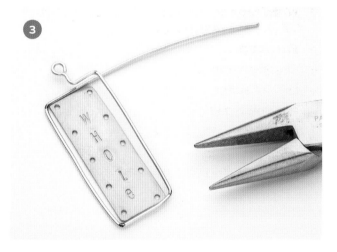

6. Wrap the short tail of the wire that remains around the area just below the simple loop. This is tricky because the two top corners are going to want to come closer together when wrapping the wire around the loop. To avoid that, hold the wire frame in the jaws of the chain-nose pliers and wrap the wire by hand. If that doesn't work, I found that a spool of washi paper tape or transparent tape is just the right size to wedge into the frame and hold those corners apart while wrapping. Trim the excess wire with flush cutters and file if necessary. Repeat Steps 4–6 to make a second frame.

7. Slightly flatten the wire frame with the flat end of the chasing hammer. It doesn't take much to flatten it, and doing so work-hardens the wire, helping it maintain its shape.

8. Holding a metal plate in the center of a wire frame, push about 3" (7.5 cm) of a 2' (61 cm) piece of 24-gauge wire through the top right hole, passing it from the front to the back. The longer end on the front side of the work will be called the working wire; the short end on the back of the work is called the tail wire. Wrap the working wire around the edge of the frame and up through the top right hole. Do the same thing again, through the same hole so there are 2 stitches holding the plate onto the corner. Guide the working wire down to the hole below and repeat the double wrapping before moving on to the next hole. Continue until you reach the top left hole (Figure 4).

9. Wrap the working wire around the frame three times after the last stitches. Trim the excess wire. Go back to the beginning of the stitches and wrap the tail wire around the frame three times as well and trim the excess wire.

10. Add an ear wire to the loop at the top of each earring.

11. Oxidize in liver of sulfur and very hot water; very hot water makes the two different metals oxidize at the same time. Remove the excess oxidation with a polishing pad.

Resources

Sterling wire, copper sheet metal or strip: riogrande.com. Washi paper tape: joann.com.

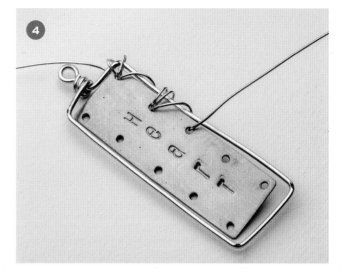

Enchanted

Cassie Donlen

Materials

+ 8½" (21.5 cm) of 10-gauge round sterling silver wire

+ 7" (18 cm) of 16-gauge round sterling silver wire

+ ¾" (2 cm) of 16-gauge round fine silver wire

+ One 4.5mm sterling silver jump ring

+ One 1⅛" (2.9 cm) red enamel heart

Tools

+ Chasing hammer

+ Steel bench block

+ Metal file

+ Fine-point Sharpie marker

+ 2-hole screw-down hole punch

+ Ball-peen hammer

+ Butane micro torch

+ Charcoal soldering block

+ Fireproof work surface (cookie sheet)

+ Utility pliers

+ Quenching bowl

+ Steel bracelet mandrel

+ Rawhide mallet

+ Flat-nose pliers

+ Letter / from an alphabet stamping set

+ Wire cutters

+ Riveting hammer

+ Round-nose pliers

+ Liver of sulfur

+ 0000 fine steel wool

Finished size

+ 2⅝" (6.7 cm)

1. Use a chasing hammer to flatten each end of the 10-gauge wire into a paddle shape. It needs to be flat and wide enough to accommodate a ¹⁄₁₆" (2 mm) punched hole. Smooth and round the edges with a metal file.

2. Use a Sharpie marker to place a dot on both flattened paddles in the center about 3 mm from the edge. Make a hole at each dot with the smaller ¹⁄₁₆" (2 mm) size of a 2-hole screw-down hole punch.

3. To texture the wire, use the round end of a ball-peen hammer to gently place marks in the wire. This will help form the wire into more of a square shape. Anneal, quench, and dry the wire.

4. Shape the wire around a bracelet mandrel to form a bangle shape. If needed, use a rawhide mallet to help form the proper shape. Remove the bangle from the mandrel and continue to shape the ends so that the holes align. Use flat-nose pliers to get the proper curvature in this section. If more texturing is desired,

place the bangle on the mandrel and use the letter I from an alphabet stamping set to stamp horizontal lines on the outer edge.

5. Place the ¾" (2 cm) piece of 16-gauge fine silver wire on a charcoal block and use a micro torch to ball up one end. To get enough heat for the 16-gauge wire to ball, hold the wire with utility pliers so it is just about touching the charcoal block. The charcoal block will reflect heat onto the wire, increasing the melting temperature. Let the wire cool. Insert the wire through the aligned holes on the bangle so that the balled end sits firmly against the outer edge. Trim the wire end so that about ¹⁄₁₆" (2 mm) of wire sticks out of the hole. Place the bangle on a steel bench block and use a riveting hammer to form a rivet (see page 44).

6. Cut two 3½" (9 cm) pieces of 16-gauge sterling wire. Use round-nose pliers to form a loop on one end of the wire. Use your fingers to coil the wire around the

bangle to make about 5 coils. The coiled part should start by the riveted end of the bangle. Trim any extra wire and flatten it down. Use flat-nose pliers to push down on the coils to make the wire stay in place. Repeat on the opposite side with the other 3½" (9 cm) piece of wire.

7. Oxidize the bracelet in liver of sulfur; rinse and dry. Use fine steel wool to remove the excess patina and produce an antique silver finish.

8. Use a jump ring to attach the enameled heart to one of the looped ends on the coiled wire on the bangle; close the jump ring.

Resources

Silver: riogrande.com.
Red enamel heart: cassiedonlen.etsy.com.

Bubbles
Denise Peck

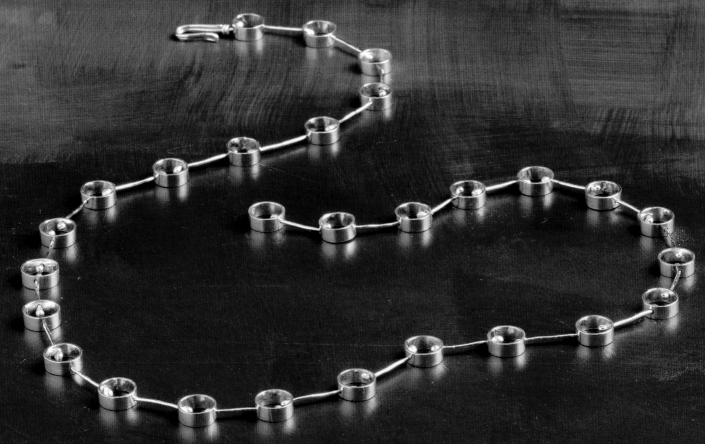

Materials

+ 30" (76 cm) of 18-gauge sterling wire
+ 28 sterling 9.5mm beads (bead frames)

Tools

+ Butane micro torch
+ Annealing pan with pumice stone
+ Fireproof work surface (cookie sheet)
+ Utility pliers

+ Quenching bowl
+ Ruler
+ Flush cutters
+ Chain-nose pliers
+ Round-nose pliers
+ Pickle
+ Mini crock
+ Copper tongs
+ Rotary tumbler
+ Mixed stainless steel shot

Finished size

+ 25" (63.5 cm)

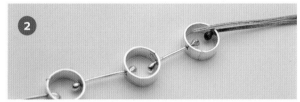

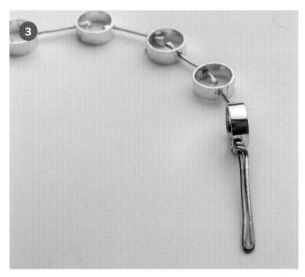

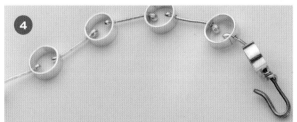

1. Working from the spool, thread the end of the wire through one hole in the ring. Slide the ring out of the way and ball the end of the wire with the torch (see page 25) (Figure 1). Quench and dry.

2. Pull the ball end of the wire against the inside of the ring. Measure ¾" (2 cm) from the ball and cut the wire.

3. Thread a second ring onto the ¾" (2 cm) wire, pushing the wire to the outside of the ring. Holding the rings as far as possible from the flame, ball the second end of the wire (Figure 2).

4. Repeat Steps 1–3 until you have 28 rings connected into a chain.

5. Cut 3" (7.5 cm) of wire, ball the end, quench, and dry. Thread it through the second hole on an end ring. Pull the ball end of the wire against the inside of the ring and mark the wire 1¼" (3.2 cm) from the ball end. Fold the wire back on itself at the mark, like a hairpin, pinching the wires together with chain-nose pliers.

6. Wrap the longer end of the wire around the base of the wire near the ring and cut off the excess (Figure 3).

7. Using round-nose pliers, fold the hairpin wire into a hook (Figure 4).

8. Pickle (see page 23), rinse, and dry. Tumble for 1 hour to polish and work-harden.

Resources
Sterling ring beads (bead frames): singharajaimports.com.

Camelot

Jane Dickerson

Materials

+ 15mm ocean blue rhinestone round
+ Scalloped raw brass collar
+ 24-gauge brass sheet
+ Etched nickel silver sheet with blue/green patina
+ 7 brass $\frac{1}{16}$" (2 mm) shank diameter × $\frac{9}{32}$" (7.1 mm) long micro screws
+ 7 brass 4mm micro nuts
+ Two 6½" (16.5 cm) lengths of brass 4mm rolo chain
+ Brass toggle clasp
+ 4 brass 7mm jump rings

Tools

+ Sheet of paper
+ Disc cutter
+ 1.8 mm metal hole-punch pliers
+ 100/180 coarse salon board
+ Ruler
+ Fine-point Sharpie marker
+ Bar Keepers Friend powder
+ Scotch-Brite green scrub pad
+ Solderite pad
+ Fireproof work surface (cookie sheet)
+ Butane micro torch
+ Utility pliers
+ Quenching bowl
+ Soft cloth
+ Renaissance Wax
+ Ball-peen hammer
+ Spiral metal stamp
+ Steel bench block

+ Eyeglass repair mini screwdriver
+ Flat- or chain-nose pliers
+ Heavy-duty flush cutters
+ Polishing pad
+ Riveting hammer
+ E6000 adhesive

Finished length

+ 19" (48.5 cm)

1. Place the paper over the front of the etched sheet and place it paper side down in the disc cutter. This will protect the etched surface from any grease on the cutter. Cut one ¾" (2 cm) disc, two ½" (1.3 cm) discs, two $\frac{1}{16}$" (1.1 cm) discs, and two ⅜" (1 cm) discs, moving the metal each time to cut the holes close together to maximize the use of your metal.

2. Using the disc cutter, cut six ¼" (6 mm) discs from the brass sheet.

3. Make a hole in the middle of each of the discs with the 1.8 mm hole-punch pliers. File the back of each disc with the salon board to remove the rough edges from the punched hole. Place the largest etched disc in the middle of the scalloped collar and, spacing the discs evenly, place each of the smaller discs in descending size order to the left and right of the center disc.

4. Once the discs are lined up, make a mark through the hole in each disc with a Sharpie, placing a dot on the brass collar beneath. Remove the discs. Punch a hole at each mark with the 1.8mm hole-punch pliers. File the back of the collar, if necessary, to remove the rough edges from the punched holes.

5. Clean the front of the brass collar with the Bar Keepers Friend, water, and a green scrub pad, working in a circular motion. Rinse and dry.

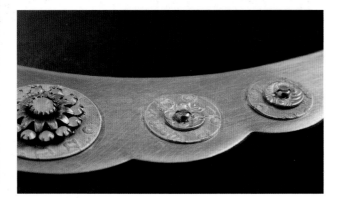

6. Place the Solderite pad on top of the cookie sheet and place the collar on top, face side up. Using the micro torch, patina the collar with the flame (see page 50). Once you have reached a color you like, quench, and dry. Seal the patina with Renaissance Wax.

7. Using a ball-peen hammer and spiral metal stamp, texture the front of the small brass discs on the steel bench block. Seal all 13 discs with Renaissance Wax.

8. Insert a micro screw through the hole in the front of the largest ¾" (2 cm) etched disc, then through the center hole of the collar. Thread a nut onto the screw and tighten with the mini screwdriver and flat- or chain-nose pliers. Trim the screw with heavy-duty flush cutters to 1⁄16" (2 mm) above the nut. Place a polishing pad over the front of the disc and place it face down on the steel bench block. Use the chisel face of the riveting hammer to gently flare the end of the screw (see Riveting with a Nail-Head Rivet, page 44), then use the flat side of the hammer to flatten it. Turn the collar over and carefully flatten the front of the screw.

9. Insert a micro screw through the front of a ¼" (6 mm) brass disc (the next smallest etched disc) and the next hole in the collar. Screw on the nut, trim the screw, and rivet back of the screw as in Step 7; do not hammer the front of the screw. Repeat until all the discs are attached.

10. Glue the rhinestone round to the center disc with E6000 adhesive. Attach one length of chain to one end of the collar with a jump ring. Attach half of the clasp to the other end of the chain with another jump ring. Repeat to attach the chain and other half of the clasp to the other side of the necklace.

Resources

Etched sheet: theartfloozy.etsy.com. Brass collar, rhinestone round, rolo chain, 1.8 mm metal hole-punch pliers, micro screws/nuts, Renaissance Wax: objectsandelements.com. Pepetools disc cutter, brass sheet, heavy-duty flush cutters: beaducation.com. E6000: michaels.com. Blazer micro torch, Solderite pad: riogrande.com.

Loose
Change

Keirsten Giles

Materials

+ 26-gauge copper and brass sheet
+ 24-gauge copper and brass sheet
+ 6" (15 cm) of 14-gauge copper wire
+ 12" (30.5 cm) of 16-gauge copper wire
+ 4" (10 cm) of 18-gauge copper wire
+ 6½' (2 m) of 22-gauge copper wire
+ Two 9×14mm lampwork beads
+ 20 amber 7×12mm oval beads
+ 12 cobalt blue 4mm "glass tile" round beads
+ 2" (5 cm) of 5mm oval brass chain
+ 6 metal 2mm crimp tubes (optional)
+ Two 24" (61 cm) pieces of ⅜" (1 cm) wide deertan leather lacing
+ 2 copper ¼" (6.5 mm) long 1.5 mm flat-head rivets
+ 2 brass ¼" (6.5 mm) long 1.5 mm flat-head rivets

Tools

+ Template
+ Disc cutter
+ Metal file
+ Butane micro torch
+ Annealing pan with pumice stone
+ Utility pliers
+ Quenching bowl
+ Pickle
+ Mini crock
+ Copper tongs
+ 0000 steel wool
+ 1" (2.5 cm) diameter coins
+ Painter's tape
+ Utility ball-peen hammer
+ Steel bench block
+ Ruler
+ Fine-tip Sharpie marker

+ 1.5 mm metal hole-punch pliers
+ Metal shears
+ Brass texture sheets
+ Heavy-duty flush cutters
+ Riveting hammer
+ Large bail-forming pliers (7 mm)
+ 2 pairs of chain-nose pliers
+ Flush cutters
+ Medium bail-forming pliers (3 mm)
+ Texturing hammer (optional)
+ Dapping block and punches
+ Oxidizer for copper and brass
+ Round-nose pliers
+ Fine- and ultrafine-grit sandpaper
+ Rotary tumbler
+ Mixed stainless steel shot
+ Stepped forming pliers (1.75–8mm)
+ Nylon-jaw pliers
+ Flat-nose pliers
+ Nylon or plastic hammer

Finished length

+ 32½" (82.5 cm)

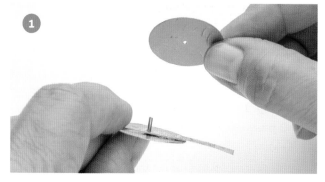

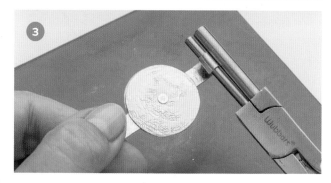

1. Cut two 1" (2.5 cm) 24-gauge copper discs and two 1" (2.5 cm) 24-gauge brass discs with the disc cutter. File the edges smooth. Anneal, quench, pickle, and dry, then clean with steel wool.

2. Texture each disc with 1" (2.5 cm) diameter coins (see page 29).

3. Mark the exact center of one copper disc and one brass disc with the Sharpie. Pair the marked copper disc with the unmarked brass disc, smooth sides together, and make a hole through both coins at the mark with the hole-punch pliers. Do the same with the marked brass disc and the remaining unmarked copper disc.

4. Cut two 7 × 50 mm strips of copper or brass from 24-gauge sheet. Anneal, quench, pickle, dry, and clean. Texture with brass texture sheets or coins.

5. Punch a hole at the exact center of each strip with the hole-punch pliers. Place a strip between a copper/brass disc set with textured sides out. Insert a brass rivet through the front of the copper disc, front of the strip, and back of the brass disc (shown here in all copper) (Figure 1). Trim the end of the brass rivet to about 2 mm and flare the end with the riveting hammer (see page 44) (Figure 2). Repeat for the other copper/brass disc set.

6. Using the 7 mm barrel of the large bail-forming pliers and flush cutters, make 4 jump rings (see page 40) from 14-gauge copper wire. Close the jump rings and hammer to flatten them slightly. Wrap each seam with about 3" (7.5 cm) of 22-gauge copper wire, wrapping about seven times around.

7. With the 3 mm barrel of the medium bail-forming pliers, curl each protruding strip over partway (Figure 3) and insert a connector ring from Step 6. Curl the strip the rest of the way over the ring and tuck the edge of the strip in between the coins (Figure 4). Do this for all 4 protruding strips and the 4 connector rings.

8. Cut two ½" (1.3 cm) discs from the 24-gauge brass sheet with the disc cutter. Texture the discs with a brass texture sheet, coin, or texturing hammer. Make a hole in the center of each disc with the hole-punch pliers.

9. With the textured side out, dome the discs with a dapping set. Oxidize and polish. Set aside.

10. Cut two 6" (15 cm) pieces of 16-gauge copper wire. Create loops with the 3 mm barrel of the medium bail-forming pliers at one end of each piece and hammer the loops lightly.

11. Slide a lampwork bead onto each piece of wire, place a brass bead cap from Step 8 on top of each, and fasten it to the bottom connector ring (if the coin focals have an "up" and "down") with a wrapped loop. (If there is too much play in the bead, slide a few 2mm metal crimps inside the bead to tighten the fit.)

12. Make 34 copper 2" (5 cm) ball-end head pins with the torch (see page 25), using 22-gauge wire. Pickle, clean, then oxidize and clean again.

13. Attach a 1" (2.5 cm) length of oval brass chain to the bottom loop under each lampwork bead. Using the head pins, attach 6 round beads to the bottom 2 chain links on each coin focal using wrapped loops. Attach 10 oval beads to the remaining chain links on each focal using wrapped loops (Figure 5).

14. Cut two Leather Rivet Ends from 26-gauge copper sheet using the template on page 140. Anneal, quench, pickle, and dry, then clean with steel wool. Texture each Leather Rivet End with brass texture sheets or coins. Round the corners with the shears and then sand all the edges with fine- and then ultrafine-grit sandpaper. You do not need to re-anneal. Oxidize and tumble, or hand-polish, now as you won't be able to do this after it is fastened to the leather.

15. Create 2 copper 3" (7.5 cm) ball-end head pins from 18-gauge wire. Oxidize. Lightly hammer the balls to flatten them. Set aside.

16. Mark the center of each Leather Rivet End from Step 13 with the Sharpie. Make a hole at each mark with the hole-punch pliers. Grasp each piece, with

the smooth side facing you, at the center where the hole is with the 1.75 mm barrel of the stepped forming pliers. Fold the rectangle gently into a wide V, with the textured side on the outside. The hole you made should be sitting right over the fold.

17. Insert a flattened ball-end head pin into the hole in one Leather Rivet End, with the ball inside the V (Figure 6). Keeping the flattened ball tight up against the inside of the V, bring the two sides almost together. Insert both pieces of the leather lacing, rough sides together, into the V, pushing it up as far as it will go,

7

8

punch pliers, going all the way through both sides of the metal and the leather.

19. Insert a flat-head copper rivet and trim the straight protruding end to about 2 mm above the metal. Flare the ends with a riveting hammer, being sure to keep the leather straight (Figure 7).

20. Create a wrapped loop with the protruding length of the head pin, fastening it to the connector ring on one of the coins before wrapping it closed. Repeat Steps 17–20 for the other end of the leather and the other coin focal.

21. Cut two 30 × 10 mm pieces of 26-gauge brass sheet. Anneal, quench, pickle, and dry, then clean them with steel wool. Texture with brass texture sheets or coins (the final dimensions will be slightly larger if you use this texturing technique). Round the corners with the shears and then sand all the edges with fine- and then ultrafine-grit sandpaper. Oxidize and polish.

22. With the smooth side facing you, bend the edges up 10 mm in from each side with flat-nose pliers and slide them onto the leather 8" (20.5 cm) from each end. Bend the edges the rest of the way over the leather and tap lightly with a nylon or plastic hammer to tighten (Figure 8).

Resources

Deertan lacing: leathercordUSA.com. Amber ovals, cobalt blue 4mm "glass tile" beads: firemountaingems .com. Copper and brass rivets: orrtec.etsy.com. Metal sheet: monsterslayer.com. Wubbers bail-forming pliers, stepped forming pliers, oxidizer: riogrande.com. Coins: joelscoins.com.

and bring the sides of the V together. Squeeze the V together gently over the leather with the nylon-jaw pliers, being sure to keep the edges of the metal flush with each other and the leather straight. You may use a bit of glue at this time if you like to keep the leather in place until you are ready to rivet it, but it is not necessary. If you use a bit of glue to hold the leather in place, let it dry.

18. Make a mark with the Sharpie on one side of the metal, centered and about 4 mm from the rounded, cut edge. Make a hole at the mark with the hole-

Silk Road

Keirsten Giles

CONES:
Materials

+ 30-gauge copper sheet
+ 36" (91.5 cm) of 18-gauge copper wire
+ 6" (15 cm) of 16-gauge copper wire
+ 10mm faceted red agate bead
+ 10mm carnelian nugget
+ 7 assorted moss agate beads
+ Jumbo burned-horn bead cap (bead cup)
+ 12" (30.5 cm) of antique copper petite steampunk chain

Finished cone lengths

+ Large cone: 40 mm; small cone: 25 mm

TUBE BAIL:
Materials

+ 24- or 26-gauge copper sheet
+ 36" (91.5 cm) of 20-gauge copper wire
+ 10–15 carnelian 6–7.5mm nuggets
+ 1 tube of size 6° amber seed beads
+ 1 moss agate 4×12mm tube bead
+ Sari silk ribbon
+ 36" (91.5 cm) of waxed linen cord
+ 12" (30.5 cm) of antique copper 5mm copper rolo chain
+ $\frac{5}{32}$" × $\frac{3}{32}$" (4 × 2.4 mm) eyelet
+ 2 antique copper 6mm jump rings
+ 2 antique copper 8mm jump ring
+ Antique copper S-clasp and ring

Finished bail length

+ 21½" (54.5 cm)

Tools*

+ Metal shears
+ Metal file
+ Butane micro torch
+ Annealing pan with pumice stone
+ Fireproof work surface (cookie sheet)
+ Utility pliers
+ Quenching bowl
+ Pickle
+ Mini crock
+ Copper tongs
+ 0000 steel wool
+ Brass texture sheet or coin
+ Painter's tape
+ Heavy utility hammer
+ Steel bench block
+ Fine- and ultrafine-grit sandpaper
+ Liver of sulfur
+ Rotary tumbler
+ Mixed stainless steel shot

*Additional Tools for Cone

+ Round-nose pliers
+ Chain-nose pliers
+ ¼" (6 mm) center punch
+ $\frac{5}{16}$" (8 mm) center punch
+ Nylon mallet
+ 15.4 mm and 9.1 mm dapping punches

*Additional Tools for Bail

+ Ruler
+ Fine-point Sharpie marker
+ Straight edge
+ Square/flat-nose pliers
+ Vise (optional)
+ 11 mm round mandrel
+ 2-hole screw-down punch
+ Center punch
+ Chasing hammer
+ Pro-Polish pad (optional)
+ Scissors

Cones

1. Using the Silk Road large cone template on page 140, cut out the piece from 30-gauge sheet with metal shears and file the edges smooth. Anneal, quench, pickle, and dry the piece, then clean it with steel wool. Texture with a brass texture sheet or coin (see page 29). Anneal again, quench, pickle, dry, and clean with steel wool.

2. With the textured side facing you, use round-nose pliers to grasp one of the wider corners along the bottom edge. Form a curl, curling the textured side back over on itself. Curl until the top edge of the curl is about two-thirds of the way up the cone (Figure 1).

3. To form the cylinder shape, grasp the top narrow edge of the cone with round-nose pliers. Bend the sides up over the round jaw of the pliers, keeping the smooth side inside. With the round-nose pliers still inserted into the top of the half-formed cone, use your fingers to mold the noncurled edge over the round jaw of the pliers, then with your fingers bring the curled side over the top of the flat side. Continue to shape with your fingers and pliers until you have a round opening at the top about 4 mm across (Figure 2).

4. Insert a conical-shaped tool (such as a large cone-shaped center punch) at the larger end and, with your fingers, begin forming the bottom edges into a cone shape. Be sure to maintain the flare of the cone, with a wider opening at the bottom and the small opening at the top. Use round-nose pliers to finalize the cone shape at the top (Figures 3 and 4).

5. Insert a 15.4 mm dapping punch into the large end of the cone to keep the rounded shape and tap the vertical edge lightly with a nylon hammer to smooth it (Figure 5). Insert the top of the jumbo burned-horn bead cap into the bottom of the cone and tighten the cone if necessary so the bead cap will fit snugly. Remove the bead cap.

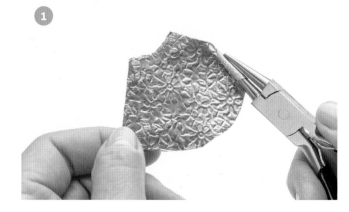

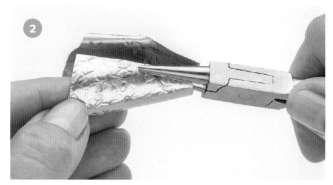

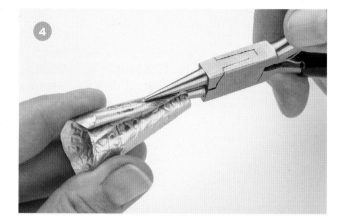

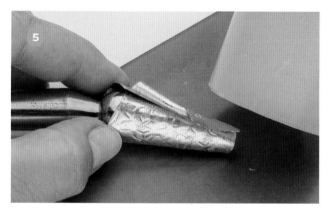

6. When you're satisfied with the shape, sand the top and bottom openings of the cone with fine and then ultra-fine-grit sandpaper until smooth. Oxidize and tumble.

7. Repeat Steps 1–6 with the Small Cone template on page 140 for the small cones (except there is no bead cap for these). If you are going to use a pair of small cones in the same piece, you may wish to have the curls be opposite each other. The smaller opening on a small cone will be 4 mm, the larger opening about 10 mm. I use the ball of my 9.1 mm dapping punch to round the larger end.

8. Make a simple loop on the end of the 16-gauge wire that just fits inside the horn bead cap enough to be hidden; you want it big enough to just fit.

9. Make 8 ball-end 18-gauge head pins with the torch (see page 25): six 2" (5 cm) long and two 3" (7.5 cm) long. String the 2 large moss agate beads onto the 3" (7.5 cm) head pins and carefully hammer the wire above the bead with the chasing hammer to flatten it. String the remaining moss agate and carnelian beads onto the remaining head pins and set aside.

10. String one end of the chain onto the 16-gauge simple loop, insert the wire into the bead cap and pull the loop up inside the bead cap. Measure the chain so it shows below the bead cap then cut 6 assorted lengths that will be long enough to show. Trim the 3" (7.5 cm) head pins to slightly different lengths and form a simple loop at the top of each. String 3 of the lengths of chain onto the 16-gauge simple loop, then the 3" (7.5 cm) head pins (now eye pins), and then 3 more lengths of chain. Begin a wrapped loop on each of the 6 head pins from Step 9, attaching each one to the end of a length of chain before completing the wrap.

11. Thread the 16-gauge wire through the bead cap and push the bead cap into the large cone, pulling the wire up through the top of the cone. Create a simple loop at the top of the cone.

Tube Bail

1. Using the Silk Road tube bail template on page 140, cut out the piece from 24- or 26-gauge sheet with metal shears and file the edges smooth. Anneal, quench, pickle, and dry the piece, then clean it with steel wool.

2. Texture the piece with a brass texture sheet or coin (see page 29). Anneal again, quench, pickle, and dry, then clean with steel wool. Clean up any irregularities in the edges caused by the texturing process with a metal file and fine- or ultrafine-grit sandpaper.

3. With the textured side up, draw lines across the ends 10 mm in from the each end with the Sharpie. With the textured side still facing you, use a straightedge, vise, or square- or flat-nose pliers to bend the ends up at the lines to a 90° angle (Figure 1).

4. Bend the piece around the mandrel, with the textured side on the outside and the smooth side against the tool, until the bent ends meet. Fold the rounded ends down until they touch, completing the bail.

5. Make a $^3/_{32}$" (2.4 mm) hole with the 2-hole screw-down punch at the bottom center of the hanging portions, about 3 mm from the bottom edge, just big enough for the eyelet. Insert the eyelet and flare the back (see page 45) (Figure 2).

6. Even the edges of the bail as necessary with the file and finish the edges with fine-grit and then ultrafine-grit sandpaper until smooth. Oxidize and tumble or hand-polish the piece.

Assembling the Necklace

1. Attach the simple loop at the top of the cone to the riveted hole at the bottom of the bail. Use 18-gauge wire to make a multilayered coil around the bottom of

the simple loop and around the top of the cone. Trim the wire and pinch in the end with chain-nose pliers.

2. Cut the waxed linen into three 12" (30.5 cm) lengths. Take one strand and, leaving a 2" (5 cm) tail, make a knot. String 1 seed bead, push it down to the knot, and tie another knot next to the bead. Continue adding seed beads and knots, with about ½" (1.3 cm) between the knots, until you have about 6½" (16.5 cm) of beaded cord. Repeat for a second seed-bead strand. For the third strand, use the carnelian nuggets.

3. Cut seven 8½" (21.5 cm) lengths of sari silk ribbon. Thread the ribbons and the waxed linen strands through the bail, centering the ribbon and the beaded portion of the strands. The beaded sections should be 6½" (16.5 cm) long. Make one knot on each end with all 3 beaded strands, about ½" (1.3 cm) from where the beads end.

4. Leaving a 6" (15.2 cm) tail, wrap 20-gauge wire tightly around the ribbons and large cord knots (this will be tucked inside the small cones) on one side of the bail. Trim the wrapping wire and pinch in the ends with chain-nose pliers. Readjust the ribbons and cords through the bail and repeat this step on the other side, making sure they drape nicely. Thread each 6" (15 cm) wire through a small cone and pull the ribbons and cords inside the cone. Trim any excess ribbon or cord so it fits neatly inside the cone, then make a multilayered wrapped loop, covering the top of the cone. Use a 6mm jump ring to connect one 6" (15 cm) length of rolo chain to each wrapped loop. Connect the clasp and ring to the other ends of the chain with 8mm jump rings. Make a 2" (5 cm) ball-end head pin with 20-gauge wire (see page 25). String the moss agate tube bead onto the head pin and attach it to the clasp ring with a wrapped loop.

Cones Resources

Copper sheet: monsterslayer.com. Center punches: homedepot.com. Brass texture sheet: metalliferous.com. Coin: joelscoins.com. Chain: chaingallery.com. Carnelian nugget, red agate bead, moss agate beads: firemountaingems.com. Burned-horn jumbo bead cap (bead cup): beadsandpieces.com.

Tube Bail Resources

Copper sheet: monsterslayer.com. Brass texture sheet: metalliferous.com. Coins: joelscoins.com. Center punch/flaring tool: homedepot.com. Sari silk ribbon: jmozart.etsy.com. Waxed linen cording: whitecloverkiln.etsy.com. Carnelian nuggets: firemountaingems.com. Rolo chain: limabeads.com.

Templates

Calliope
Denise Peck, page 94.

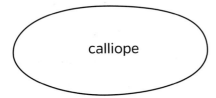

calliope

Doorknocker
Keirsten Giles, page 96.

doorknocker

Corbel
Keirsten Giles, page 104.

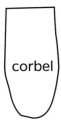

corbel

Sedona
Keirsten Giles, page 112.

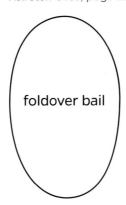

foldover bail

Loose Change
Keirsten Giles, page 129.

leather rivet ends

Silk Road
Keirsten Giles, page 134.

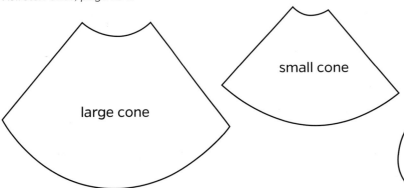

large cone

small cone

tube bail

Resources

Ace Hardware **acehardware.com**

Antelope Beads **antelopebeads.com**

Art Floozy **theartfloozy.etsy.com**

Beads and Pieces
beadsandpieces.com

Beaducation Inc. **beaducation.com**

Bed Bath and Beyond
bedbathandbeyond.com

B'Sue Boutiques
bsueboutiques.com

Cascadia Beads
cascadiabeads.etsy.com

Cassie Donlen
cassiedonlen.etsy.com

Chain Gallery **chaingallery.com**

Coiling Gizmo **coilinggizmo.com**

Crafted Findings
craftedfindings.com

Do It Best **doitbest.com**

East West DyeCom **eastwestdye.com**

eBay **ebay.com**

Echo Artworks Bead Shop and Gallery
echoartworks.com

Fiber Goddess **fibergoddess.net**

Fire Mountain Gems and Beads
firemountaingems.com

Fusion Beads **fusionbeads.com**

Gem Mall **gemmall.com**

Gulnur Ozdaglar
gulnurozdaglar.etsy.com

Harbor Freight Tools
harborfreight.com

Helby Import Company
(The BeadSmith) **helby.com**

Home Depot **homedepot.com**

JewelrySupply **jewelrysupply.com**

Jo-Ann Fabric and Craft Stores
joann.com

Joel Anderson **joelscoins.com**

Kabela Design **kabeladesign.com**

Leather Cord USA
leathercordusa.com

Lillypilly Designs Inc.
lillypillydesigns.com

Lima Beads **limabeads.com**

Melinda Orr Designs **orrtec.etsy.com**

Melissa Manley
melissamanley.etsy.com

Metalliferous **metalliferous.com**

Michaels **michaels.com**

MonsterSlayer **monsterslayer.com**

Mudhound Studio Mixed Media
jmozart.etsy.com

Objects and Elements
objectsandelements.com

Ornamentea **ornamentea.com**

Otto Frei **ottofrei.com**

Paramount Wire Co. **parawire.com**

Patina Queen **patinaqueen.etsy.com**

PJ Tool & Supply **pjtool.com**

Rio Grande **riogrande.com**

Santa Fe Jewelers Supply
sfjssantafe.com

Silk Road Treasures
silkroadtreasures.com

Singaraja Imports
singarajaimports.com

T. B. Hagstoz and Son Inc.
hagstoz.com

Thunderbird Supply Company
thunderbirdsupply.com

The Urban Beader **urbanbeader.com**

Vintaj **vintaj.com**

White Clover Kiln
whitecloverkiln.etsy.com

Windspirit **windspirit.etsy.com**

Wired Arts **wiredarts.net**

Wire-Sculpture.com
wire-sculpture.com

Wubbers **wubbers.com**

Bibliography

Bogert, Kerry. *Totally Twisted: Innovative Wirework & Art Glass Jewelry*. Loveland, Colorado: Interweave, 2009.

———. *Rustic Wrappings: Exploring Patina in Wire, Metal, and Glass Jewelry*. Loveland, Colorado: Interweave, 2012.

Bombardier, Jodi. *Weave, Wrap, Coil: Creating Artisan Wire Jewelry*. Loveland, Colorado: Interweave, 2010.

Bone, Elizabeth. *Silversmithing for Jewelry Makers: A Handbook of Techniques and Surface Treatments*. Loveland, Colorado: Interweave, 2012.

Driggs, Helen. *The Jewelry Maker's Field Guide: Tools and Essential Techniques*. Loveland, Colorado: Interweave, 2013.

Hettmansperger, Mary. *Heat, Color, Set & Fire: Surface Effects for Metal Jewelry*. New York: Lark Crafts, 2012.

Kazmer, Susan Lenart. *15+ Ways to Alter Metal Surfaces: Cold Enameling, Resin, Powders, Pastels, and More*. DVD. Loveland, Colorado: Interweave, 2013.

Kelly, Lisa Niven. *Stamped Metal Jewelry: Techniques & Designs for Making Custom Jewelry*. Loveland, Colorado: Interweave, 2010.

Live Wire eMagazine. Loveland, Colorado: Interweave, 2011.

McCreight, Tim. *Patina Basics: Safe Color Solutions for Metalsmiths*. DVD. Brunswick, Maine: Brynmorgen Press, 2010.

Miller, Sharilyn. *Wire Art Jewelry Workshop: Step-by-Step Techniques and Projects (with DVD)*. Loveland, Colorado: Interweave, 2011.

Moore, Gail Crosman. *Coloring on Metal for Jewelry Makers*. DVD. Loveland, Colorado: Interweave, 2013.

Peck, Denise. *Wire Style: 50 Unique Jewelry Designs*. Loveland, Colorado: Interweave, 2008.

———. *Wire Style 2: 45 New Jewelry Designs (with DVD)*. Loveland, Colorado: Interweave, 2011.

Peck, Denise and Jane Dickerson. *Handcrafted Wire Findings: Techniques and Designs for Custom Jewelry Components*. Loveland, Colorado: Interweave, 2011.

———. *The Wireworker's Companion*. Loveland, Colorado: Interweave, 2013.

Wimmer, Cindy. *The Missing Link: From Basic to Beautiful Wirework Jewelry*. Loveland, Colorado: Interweave, 2013.

Young, Anastasia. *The Workbench Guide to Jewelry Techniques*. Loveland, Colorado: Interweave, 2010.

Index

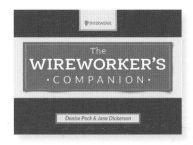